813.3
Walker, Nancy A.
Fanny Fern

LYONS PUBLIC LIBRARY

Lyons, Illinois

Fanny Fern

Twayne's United States Authors Series

Nancy A. Walker, Editor

Vanderbilt University

TUSAS 616

FANNY FERN

Sketch of Fanny Fern (Sara Willis Parton) drawn by her daughter Grace as "a very bad likeness—yet funnily like, too, in some respects."
Sophia Smith Collection, Smith College

Fanny Fern

Nancy A. Walker

Vanderbilt University

Twayne Publishers • New York
Maxwell Macmillan Canada • Toronto
Maxwell Macmillan International • New York   Oxford   Singapore   Sydney

Fanny Fern
Nancy A. Walker

Twayne Publishers   Maxwell Macmillan Canada Inc.
Macmillan Publishing Company   1200 Eglinton Avenue East
866 Third Avenue   Suite 200
New York, New York 10022   Don Mills, Ontario M3C 3N1

Macmillan Publishing Company is a member of the Maxwell Communication Group
of Companies.

Library of Congress Cataloging-in-Publication Data

Walker, Nancy A., 1942–
    Fanny Fern / Nancy A. Walker.
        p.   cm. — (Twayne's United States authors series ; TUSAS 616)
    Includes bibliographical references and index.
    ISBN 0–8057–3981–5
    1. Fern, Fanny, 1811–1872—Criticism and interpretation.
I. Title. II. Series.
PS2523.P9Z95   1993
813'.3—dc20   92–36856
                                                          CIP

10 9 8 7 6 5 4 3 2 1

For Burt and Jed,
who were quite patient with me and "Fanny";
and for Tigger and Roo,
who were not.

Contents

Preface   ix

Chronology   xiii

Chapter One
Sara Payson Willis Parton and Fanny Fern   1

Chapter Two
Sentiment and Satire: *Fern Leaves*   23

Chapter Three
Fame and Controversy: *Ruth Hall*   40

Chapter Four
Rose Clark   63

Chapter Five
"Little Ferns": Fanny Fern's Books for Children   80

Chapter Six
"A lady whom all the world knows"   99

Notes and References   123
Selected Bibliography   127
Index   131

Preface

In her book *A Day at a Time*, Margo Culley comments on women diarists' tendency to objectify their diaries as individuals to be confided in, even to the point of giving them names. Culley notes that in 1876 a young woman in New York State decided to name her diary "Fannie Fern," and subsequently confided to "Dear Fan" her youthful activities and dreams.[1] The fact that Helen Ward Brandreth chose (even if she misspelled it) the name in turn chosen by Sara Willis Parton as the pseudonym under which she wrote her popular novels and newspaper columns is one of many indications of how widely known the author was. The subject of much controversy during her career, particularly regarding her 1854 novel *Ruth Hall*, Sara Willis Parton had, by the time she died in 1872, published two novels, three books of stories for children, and hundreds of newspaper columns, many of which had been reprinted in six collections, published between 1853 and 1872. A railroad car had been named for Fanny Fern, as had a number of children.

Yet like many nineteenth-century women writers, Fanny Fern and her contributions to American literary and cultural history were subsequently pushed from view as nineteenth-century American literature became defined by critics and literary historians as featuring the work of Melville, Poe, Hawthorne, Whitman, Twain, and others who contributed to or benefitted from what F. O. Matthiessen called the "American Renaissance." More specifically, Parton/Fern became relegated, by the 1950s, to the easily dismissed group of female "domestic" novelists of the midnineteenth century, known for their sentimental, moralistic, melodramatic fiction. Even though Nathaniel Hawthorne exempted Fanny Fern from what he called the "d——d mob of scribbling women," an increasingly rigid distinction between "serious" and "popular" literature prevented scholars from seriously exploring widely read women's literature of the nineteenth century.

Indeed, when Culley's *A Day at a Time* was published in 1985, Fanny Fern's novel *Ruth Hall*—as well as the rest of her work—had been out of print for many years, and with the exception of two unpublished master's theses, her work was not the subject of scholarly attention. In 1986, however, Joyce W. Warren edited *Ruth Hall* and a selection of Fanny

Fern's newspaper columns for the Rutgers University Press American Women Writers Series. Warren's carefully researched introduction, including her analysis of *Ruth Hall*, sparked renewed interest in Fanny Fern, and constitutes the germ of my study of the writer herein. Both the reissuance of *Ruth Hall* and this volume in Twayne's United States Authors Series are part of a reconsideration of nineteenth-century American literature that has been undertaken by both historians and literary critics within the past two decades—a reconsideration that has been instigated largely by the insights of American culture studies and feminist scholarship and that has forced a revision of our understanding of the origins of realism, the interaction between fiction and society, and the role of the woman writer in a developing American literary tradition.

Fanny Fern would have understood, I think, the impulse of feminist scholars to establish women writers as creators rather than merely subjects of art. In a column titled "Try Again," included in her 1857 collection *Fresh Leaves*, she counters in an interesting way the assertion that women have not created great works of art. She first proposes women's equivalent contributions; to the statement that "No woman ever composed a great piece of music," for example, she retorts, "What do you call a baby?" Although perhaps women have not been the authors of great novels and epics, she concedes, they have certainly furnished the subject matter of those by men: "Just tell me what *your* 'letters,' *your* 'novels,' *your* 'epics,' would have amounted to without the inspiring theme—*woman*. When the world furnishes us *heroes*, perhaps *we* shall write splendid novels, splendid epics."[2] If, in other words, men were as inspiring as women, women could create great art.

This is the first full-length study of Fanny Fern. Her place in American literary history remains to be fully determined. Certainly her novel *Ruth Hall* is an important part of midnineteenth-century fiction, not only because it resists the typical formulation of the domestic novel, but also because it is a complex novel that provides a realistic view of antebellum urban life in the northeastern United States. I have devoted considerable attention to Fanny Fern's newspaper columns—primarily those collected in book form because these are available in some libraries—and to her writing for children for three reasons. First, these types of writing constituted the bulk of her 20-year career and were the way in which she reached the majority of her readers. Also, the columns and the stories for children provide excellent insights into issues important to Americans of the 1850s and 1860s—e.g., fashions, funerals, parenting, the "Woman Question," prison reform, and the educational system. Finally, the newspaper columns in particular reveal better than any other source Fanny Fern's concepts of progressive social reform, her feminist and abolitionist sympathies, her wit, and her wisdom.

I wish to express my thanks to the interlibrary loan staff at Vanderbilt University's Heard Library, who provided unfailingly prompt and courteous service, and to Caroline Woidat and Amy Lang, for their useful comments on portions of the manuscript.

Chronology

1811   Sara Payson Willis born 9 July to Nathaniel and Hannah Willis in Portland, Maine, the fifth of nine children. Six weeks later, the family moves to Boston, where Nathaniel Willis begins the first religious newspaper in America, *The Puritan Recorder*.

1827   Nathaniel Willis begins editing *The Youth's Companion* and continues until 1862.

1828–1829   Attends Catharine Beecher's Female Seminary in Hartford, Connecticut.

1829   Delivers annual Exhibition Day address at Beecher's Seminary upon her graduation: a humorous talk about her difficulties with learning arithmetic titled "Suggestions on Arithmetic."

1829–1837   Lives at home in Boston, doing domestic chores and proofreading and writing articles for her father's newspapers.

1837   Marries Charles Harrington Eldredge, a bank cashier, on 4 May.

1838   First daughter, Mary Stace, born.

1841   Second daughter, Grace Harrington, born in February.

1844   Sara's youngest sister, Ellen, dies in February; Sara's mother dies in March; Sara's third daughter, Ellen Willis, born in September.

1845   Sara's oldest daughter, Mary, dies of brain fever in March.

1846   Charles Eldredge dies of typhoid fever in October.

1849   On 15 January, marries Samuel P. Farrington at the insistence of her father; purely a marriage of convenience to provide Sara with financial support and Farrington with a mother for his two daughters, the marriage lasts only two years, although the divorce was not final until 1853.

1851   Publishes her first newspaper piece in the Boston *Olive Branch* on 18 June, for which she is paid fifty cents; in September, she begins to sign her work as "Fanny Fern."

1852   In October, "Fanny Fern's Column" begins to appear regularly in the New York paper *Musical World and Times*.

1853   Derby and Miller publish *Fern Leaves from Fanny's Port-Folio* and *Little Ferns for Fanny's Little Friends*; writes briefly for the *Saturday Evening Post*.

1854   Publishes *Fern Leaves*, Second Series; in December, Mason Brothers publishes *Ruth Hall*, and William U. Moulton, editor of the Boston *True Flag*, reveals Fanny Fern's identity.

1855   *The Life and Beauties of Fanny Fern* is anonymously published in March; signs contract with Robert Bonner, editor of the *New York Ledger*, to write for the *Ledger* at $100 per column.

1856   Marries James Parton on 5 January; in July, the couple move to Oxford Street in Brooklyn; second novel, *Rose Clark*, published.

1857   *Fresh Leaves* and *The Play-Day Book* published.

1859   Moves with husband to 303 East Eighteenth Street in Manhattan.

1863   Following the death of daughter Grace, the Partons adopt Grace's daughter Ethel.

1864   *The New Story Book for Children* published.

1868   *Folly As It Flies* published.

1870   *Ginger-Snaps* published.

1872   *Caper-Sauce* published. Dies of cancer 10 October.

Chapter One
Sara Payson Willis Parton and Fanny Fern

Although it is not uncommon for authors—especially women—to use pseudonyms, rarely does the assumed name become an identity that effectively replaces the real identity of the writer as it did in the case of Fanny Fern. Adopted by the intensely private Sara Willis as the pen name for her newspaper columns in the early 1850s, Fanny Fern was the only name carved on her tombstone when she died in 1872. As the most widely reprinted and most highly paid newspaper columnist of the 1850s, Fanny Fern was the public *persona* of the woman who, if she had retained the names of all three husbands, would have been known as Sara Payson Willis Eldredge Farrington Parton. It is perhaps not surprising that the details of the private life of a woman with so many names and identities should have been the subject of much speculation and controversy, both during her life and after her death.

The name Fanny Fern was already well-known by the time her novel *Ruth Hall* was published in 1854, but the real identity of its author (at that time legally Sara Farrington) remained a closely guarded secret. Within a few months of its publication, however, a spurious "biography" of Fanny Fern revealed her to be the daughter of publisher Nathaniel Willis and the sister of N. P. Willis, also a well-known figure in journalistic circles. Presumed now to be the work of William Moulton, editor of the Boston *True Flag*, *The Life and Beauties of Fanny Fern* portrays Sara Willis as a shrewd, self-serving opportunist rather than the talented, hardworking widow who is the title character in her highly autobiographical novel. Moulton's work thus delivered a double blow: it not only removed the veil of anonymity from Sara Willis but also impugned her character and motives. Whereas the heroine of *Ruth Hall* struggles to support her two small children without assistance from her family—eventually, as was the case in Sara Willis's own experience, becoming a successful columnist with a large number of devoted readers—Moulton declares that "no starving necessity had compelled her to resort to the pen,"[1] and takes her to task for the unflattering portraits of her relatives in *Ruth Hall*. The glare of such unfavorable publicity was especially harsh to a woman who had sought to keep her identity as an author separate from her private life, as did other women writers of the period. Historian Mary Kelley, in *Private Woman, Public Stage*, notes that public recognition posed considerable problems for the writers whom she terms "literary domestics": "Being private domestic females, the literary domestics did not find it easy to grapple with unexpected public notice, and resisted a public status that had never before befallen American women. The difficulty they experienced was more than that of attempting to separate the private from the public: they had unexpectedly been placed in the male role of public figure, a role that had not been and was not supposed to be part of the female experience."[2]

Although Sara Willis was quick to declare that *The Life and Beauties of Fanny Fern* had been written without her consultation—much less her authorization—its status as an actual biography remained largely undisputed for many years. In 1939, for example, a doctoral student at Columbia University wrote a biographical dissertation on Fanny Fern that relies heavily on Moulton's work. Though noting that this "anonymous publication" contains "several inaccuracies of fact,"[3] the dissertation's author, Mae Weintraub Zlotnik, quotes large portions of it in reconstructing the author's life. Not until Joyce W. Warren edited a republication of *Ruth Hall* and selections from Fanny Fern's newspaper columns for the Rutgers University Press American Women Writers Series in 1986 was *The Life and Beauties* publically revealed as a spiteful fabrication.

Just as the biographical details of Sara Willis/Fanny Fern's life had been the subject of debate and misunderstanding, so her place in American literary history has been obscured by the tendency of literary historians to consign her to the group of female writers of the 1850s that Nathaniel Hawthorne termed the "d——d mob of scribbling women" who wrote sentimental fiction. Until the 1970s, few would have disputed Fred Lewis Pattee's 1940 assessment of Fanny Fern as the "most tearful and convulsively 'female' moralizer" of this group.[4] To be sure, Fanny Fern was adept at using the overblown rhetoric and clichéd subjects common to the romantic fiction of her day. In the first part of her novel *Ruth Hall* and in many of her "Fern Leaves" newspaper columns, she employed the prevailing sentimental mode in writing about self-sacrificing mothers, sick children, and the consolation of religious belief; but more commonly she adopted a sprightly—at times markedly satiric—style and tone with which to comment on fads, fashions, and even topics normally considered taboo for members of either sex to address, such as prostitution, venereal disease, the sexual double standard, and women's rights. She championed Walt Whitman's *Leaves of Grass* in 1856, at a time when the term most commonly applied to Whitman's poetry was "vulgar"; writing for the *New York Ledger* in May 1856, Fanny Fern hailed Whitman as a "large-hearted, untainted, self-reliant, fearless son of the Stars and Stripes."[5] which was fitting praise from an author whom Hawthorne had earlier characterized as writing "as if the devil was in her."[6]

Fanny Fern's reputation as a sentimental writer was perpetuated not only by scholars such as Pattee, but also by her journalistic heirs. Dorothy Dix, America's first true advice columnist, briefly considered Fern as a model for her own work when she was beginning her career in the 1890s, but apparently read only the most conventional portions of *Fern Leaves*, because Dix's biographer reports that she rejected the "syrupy" quality of Fern's work.[7] Ironically, Dix's career paralleled that of Fanny Fern in several important ways. Like Sara Willis, she chose an alliterative pseudonym that became her public identity. Her newspaper columns, like those of Fanny Fern, satirized pretension and hypocrisy; she had little use for "society" and its trappings. And Dix, like Fern, was extremely popular with readers and ultimately was rewarded for her popularity: in the first decade of the twentieth century, the New York *Journal* offered her an annual salary of $13,000—the largest yet paid to a woman journalist.

In her rejection of hypocrisy and pretence and her satiric commentaries on middle-class tastes and aspirations, Fanny Fern had more in common with Walt Whitman and Mark Twain than with the "literary domestics" and "scribbling women" with whom she was grouped by generations of scholars. In addition to the dual identity of Sara Willis Parton/Fanny Fern, the latter was able to write in two different voices: one which mouthed the sentimental platitudes of the period, and another, increasingly dominant as her career progressed, that attacked satirically the very origins of naive sentimentality. Of a child whose father has recently died, Fanny Fern could write: "the winter wind sang its mournful requiem, and from out the little brown house, the orphan passed with tearful gaze and lingering footstep."[8] Yet when she unleashed her wit, such clichéd language gave way to remarkably sprightly prose. In "The Model Widower," for example, she addresses the tendency of widowers to marry women much younger than themselves:

"Begins to think of No. 2 before the weed in his hat loses its first gloss;—may be seen assisting young girls to find a seat in church . . . hangs his first wife's portrait in the attic . . . and marries a playmate of his oldest daughter."[9] It seems likely that the overwhelming success of her first two collections of sketches, *Fern Leaves from Fanny's Port-Folio* and *Fern Leaves*, Second Series, in which the more conventional tone predominates, led earlier critics to class her with the "female moralizers"; her later volumes, including *Folly As It Flies, Ginger-Snaps,* and *Caper-Sauce*, as their titles indicate, feature a higher proportion of sharp, satiric sketches.

In an October 1857 column, Fanny Fern demonstrated that she could satirize herself and at the same time take a swipe at the critics who considered her satire "unwomanly." The column is a tongue-in-cheek review of her own book, *Fresh Leaves*, published that year by Mason Brothers of New York. In a kind of ultimate self-doubling, the reviewer declares herself to be no fan of Fanny Fern's writing; she criticizes the work precisely on the grounds used to castigate her upon the publication of *Ruth Hall*: that satire was not a proper mode for a woman. The "review" reads in part: "We imagine [Fanny Fern], from her writings, to be a muscular, black-browed, grenadier-looking female, who would be more at home in a boxing gallery than in a parlor,—a vociferous, demonstrative, strong-minded horror,—a woman only by virtue of her dress. . . . When we take up a woman's book we expect to find gentleness, timidity, and that lovely reliance on the patronage of our sex which constitutes a woman's greatest charm. . . . We do not desire to see a woman wielding the scimitar blade of sarcasm."[10] Using almost the same words as her detractors, Fanny Fern—now known to the public to be Sara Willis Parton—points up the absurdity of gender stereotyping in writing.

Several years earlier, in 1853, Fanny Fern had demonstrated that she recognized and could make fun of the fashion of alliterative pseudonyms of which her own chosen name was a part. In a sketch tilted "Borrowed Light," which was included in her first *Fern Leaves* collection, she offers mock advice to the aspiring writer: "In choosing your signature, bear in mind that nothing goes down, now-a-days, but *alliteration*. For instance, Delia Daisy, Fanny Foxglove, Harriet Honeysuckle, Lily Laburnum, Paulina Poppy, Maimie Mignonette, Julia Jonquil, Seraphina Sunflower, etc., etc." (*Leaves*, 332). The central subject of "Borrowed Light" is plagiarism—the borrowing of not merely names, but also characters, plots, and language—and the essay argues, by inversion, for originality. Thus Sara Willis's selection of the name "Fanny Fern," and her subsequent adoption of this as her central identity, became complex issues for a midnineteenth-century female author.

A Proper Boston Childhood

Little in Sara Willis's family background would have predicted the several ways in which she defied convention, both personally and professionally. Her paternal ancestors were descended from Puritan settlers, the first of whom, George Willis, settled in Boston in 1630. Journalism, however, became a family tradition with Sara's grandfather, Nathaniel Willis, who edited the Boston *Independent Chronicle* during and after the American Revolution, and subsequently edited newspapers in Virginia and Ohio. Sara's father, born in Boston in 1780 and also named Nathaniel, and was apprenticed to his father at age seven, and as a young man, he returned to Boston to work in the offices of the *Independent Chronicle*. In an era in which newspapers were frequently the organs of partisan politics, Nathaniel Willis's experience on the *Independent Chronicle*, originally a Whig newspaper, made him a good candidate to start a newspaper in Portland, Maine, that would counter the Federalist views of the *Portland Gazette*. Thus in 1803, at age 23, Nathaniel Willis became the editor of the *Eastern Argus* in Portland.

In the same year that he began the *Eastern Argus* for the Democratic–Republican party of Maine, Nathaniel Willis married Hannah Parker, a woman remembered by her children as a kind and devoted mother—qualities that she no doubt found useful in raising her nine children. By the time Sara was born on 9 July 1811—the fifth of these nine and the fourth daughter—the family was undergoing financial difficulty. Nathaniel Willis, having apparently entered into the political controversies of the early Republic with gusto, was involved in several libel suits, and at one point was jailed for several months for defaulting on a $2,000 damage claim.[11] Willis's involvement with the potentially libelous form of political journalism was severely curtailed when he came under the influence of the Reverend Edward Payson, who arrived in Portland in 1807 and quickly gained a reputation for his oratorial skills. By 1808, Nathaniel Willis had sold his interest in the *Eastern Argus* and gone into the less lucrative grocery business. His journalistic ambitions, coupled with his religious convictions, prompted him to attempt to start a religious newspaper in Maine, but the political tensions surrounding the War of 1812 delayed the realization of this dream until 1816, when he began the *Boston Recorder*, the country's first religious newspaper, in the city of his ancestors.

The importance of religion in the Willis family is evidenced in the naming of the family's fifth child. She was originally christened Grata Payson Willis, Grata being the name of Edward Payson's mother. The first name was later changed to Sara, an event that foreshadowed the multiple identities that Sara would have in adult life. The combination of strict religious upbringing and the conservative nature of "proper" Bostonians seemed to have encouraged Sara's satiric impulses far more than it led her to be devout. In *Ruth Hall* she exposes religious hypocrisy, and in several of her newspaper columns she satirized Boston propriety. In one of the articles collected in *Fresh Leaves* (1857), she includes religious smugness as part of the overall "respectability" of the Bostonian: "The Boston male is respectable all over; from the crown of his glossy hat to the soles of his shiny shoes; and huggeth his mantle of self-esteem inseparably about him, that he may avoid contaminating contact with the non-elect of his 'set.' . . . [He] is conservative as a citizen, prosaic as a lover; hum-drum as a husband and has no sins—*to speak of.*"[12] Although she missed being born in Boston by a mere six weeks, Sara—or rather, Fanny Fern—later announced her gratitude that she was not technically a native of the city because she had not been "born in the beautiful, back-biting, sanctimonious, slandering, clean, contumelious, pharisaical, phiddle-de-dee, peck measure city—of Boston" (*FL*, 256).

That Nathaniel Willis was concerned with the proper religious upbringing of children is amply underscored by his establishment, in 1827, of *The Youth's Companion*, a religious newspaper for children that grew out of a children's section in the *Boston Recorder*. Willis edited *The Youth's Companion* until 1862, and the publication lasted well into the twentieth century. The Willis household in Boston was visited frequently by members of the clergy and church leaders; Nathaniel Willis himself was a deacon of the Park Street Church. Yet from childhood Sara was resistant to the atmosphere of piety. James Parton, her third husband, recalled that from childhood on she was "something of a rebel against the leading doctrine of the orthodox church . . . She found herself unable to believe either that she was a depraved sinner, or that she was in any danger of everlasting perdition. . . . Nature had not formed her a saint and the attempt to make her one was but partially successful" (*MV*, 28, 31). Inheriting his ancestors' belief that the parents' responsibility is to provide religious instruction for their children in order to curb their natural instincts for sinful behavior, Nathaniel Willis could be stern and forbidding—especially to Sara. As Florence Bannard Adams states, "It was Sara who, of all the children, was most dangerously inclined to levity and most perilously unimpressed by her sinful state. This presented a fearful problem to the uncompromising Deacon."[13]

Much of what is known about the childhood and early adolescence of Sara Willis comes from the pen of Fanny Fern, writing for the *New York Ledger* from the late 1850s through the early 1870s. Even allowing for selective memory, the young Sara was no doubt a lively tomboy who chafed against the restrictive atmosphere of her upbringing. In August 1859, for example, she wrote of "the distasteful and barbarous routine of being routed out of bed to attend long recitation and prayers before breakfast." She also recalled being punished for whispering to a fellow student in class and never forgot her distaste at being required to kiss visitors to the Willis home. In her 5 April 1862 *Ledger* column she writes of "the horror with which I looked forward, in my childhood, to the periodical visits of a snuffy old person. I think my compromising hatred of tobacco dates back to those forced snuffy kisses."

Deacon Willis was as concerned about the proper education of his children as he was about their religious devotion. The Willis boys were groomed to attend Yale University, and the girls were sent to female seminaries that combined religious instruction with education in intellectual and domestic skills. Sara's resistance to the piety and obedience expected of young ladies seems to have made her a special case to be reckoned with, and she attended several schools, including one in Lynn, Massachusetts, before going to Catharine Beecher's seminary in Hartford, Connecticut.

Catharine Beecher and Sara Willis had much in common. Both were daughters of strict, latter-day Calvinists who were deeply concerned about the spiritual well-being of their large families (Catharine had ten brothers and sisters). Lyman Beecher, who held pastorates in Litchfield, Connecticut, and in Boston as well as serving as the president of Lane Theological Seminary in Cincinnati, Ohio, functioned as a patriarch to his large clan much as did Nathaniel Willis, monitoring their intellectual and spiritual growth. But Catharine Beecher, like Sara Willis, could not accept the Calvinist doctrine of innate depravity, and so remained at odds with her father's theology. Particularly difficult for her was her father's reaction to the death of her fiancé, Alexander Fisher, who drowned while on a voyage to England in 1822. Lyman Beecher, who was concerned that Catharine had not undergone a conversion experience,

was also doubtful that Fisher had been properly prepared to meet his
maker, and so he could offer Catharine little comfort. Upon learning of
Fisher's death, Beecher wrote a letter to his daughter which reads in part
as follows: "On that which will force itself upon your pained heart with
respect to the condition of his present existence in the eternal state, I can
only say that many did and will indulge the hope that he was pious,
though without such evidence as caused him to indulge hope . . ."[14]
Fisher's death, and her father's less-than-optimistic remarks about the
state of his soul, caused Catharine to turn her back on strict Calvinist
doctrine and launch a career as a teacher. Her decision is encapsulated in
her telling remark at this time: "the heart must have *something* to rest
upon, and if it is not God, it will be the world" (*Beechers*, 53).

Catharine Beecher opened the Hartford Female Seminary in May 1823
with seven students; three years later it had almost 100 students and had
moved from a single room to a church basement. Intent upon improving
the education of young women, Beecher's school provided a curriculum
that included rhetoric, logic, natural philosophy, moral philosophy,
chemistry, history, Latin, and algebra. Despite her quarrels with her
father's Calvinism, Catharine Beecher remained a religious woman and
insisted that her teachers give attention to the students' moral and
religious development. In 1826, probably motivated more by a desire to
solidify her social status in Hartford than by religious zeal, she initiated
a religious revival both at the Hartford Female Seminary and in the city
of Hartford. On a secular level, at least, the revival was successful in
drawing attention to her educational endeavor: she was able to raise
$5,000 from the citizens of Hartford to build a new school building,
which opened in the fall of 1827 with facilities to accommodate eight
teachers and 150 students.

It was to Catharine Beecher's school that Nathaniel Willis sent Sara in
1828, on the advice of Lyman Beecher. Although it is ironic that Willis
sent his daughter to study under a woman who entertained precisely the
same religious doubts as she, the atmosphere at the Hartford Female
Seminary provided the tolerance that Sara needed in order for her talents
to be nurtured without repressing her spirit. By the time Sara entered the
seminary, Catharine's younger sister Harriet had joined the school in
the combined role of student and teacher. Although almost exactly the
same age as Sara Willis, Harriet Beecher had some supervisory responsibilities; she was the sister of the school's principal, and she taught some
of the lessons. Sara's granddaughter Ethel Parton quotes in a 1901 article
from a letter that Catharine's younger sister, by then famous as the author

of *Uncle Tom's Cabin,* wrote to James Parton. This passage clearly indicates that the school could accommodate Sara's continuing mischief:

I believe you have a claim on a certain naughty girl once called Sara Willis, in whom I still retain an interest, and who, I grieve to say, one night stole a pie at Mrs. Strong's and did feloniously excite to sedition and rebellion some five or six other girls—eating said pie between eleven and twelve o'clock in defiance of the laws of the school and in breach of the peace—*ask her* if it isn't so? and if she remembers curling her hair with leaves from her geometry?—perhaps she has long been penitent—*perhaps*—but, ah me! when I read Fanny Fern's articles I detect sparks of the old witchcraft and say, as poor Mrs. Strong [the matron] used to when any new mischief turned up, '*That's* Sara Willis, *I* know!'[15]

Harriet Beecher Stowe could have the luxury of reminiscing with delight about Sara's escapades, but at the time it was Catharine's responsibility to improve her students' deportment and spiritual commitment. In a letter to Mr. and Mrs. Willis during the time Sara was enrolled in her school, she assesses Sara's progress with cautious optimism: "I do not feel much confidence in Sara's piety; but I do feel that religious influence has greatly improved her character. She is very lovely, and though her faults are not all eradicated, and though I still fear that the World has the *first* place yet I think religion occupies much of her thoughts. She now rooms alone and has much time for reading and reflection" (*MV,* 37). One wonders whether, while writing this letter to Sara Willis's parents, Catharine Beecher recalled her own earlier decision to let her heart rest on the world rather than on God; but even if she did, she would scarcely have confessed it to the parents of one of her changes.

Much later, in one of her *New York Ledger* columns, Fanny Fern quipped that she had been sent to the Hartford Female Seminary "for algebra and safekeeping,"[16] but while she was kept reasonably safe, she seems to have had a lifelong aversion to anything mathematical. As James Parton later wrote in his *Memorial Volume of Fanny Fern,* "Her infirmity with regard to arithmetic was one from which she never recovered" (37). As might be expected, her best subject was composition, and her skill at writing, coupled with her arithmetical "infirmity," produced a comic essay about her problems with mathematics, "Suggestions on Arithmetic," which was selected to be read at the Annual Exhibition in the summer of 1829. In this, her first public foray into humor, Sara was a big success with her classmates: more than 40 years later, the daughter of one of them sent Sara a copy of her prize essay.

The essay, which foretold Fanny Fern's ability to poke fun—even at
herself—concerns her preoccupation with the dreaded mathematics, a
preoccupation so great that while walking with a young man she is
attentive to only one word of his conversation:

> Of his many speeches, one in which he protested his warm interest brought only
> one word that chimed with my train of thought. "Interest," exclaimed I,
> starting from my reverie. "What per cent, sir?" "Ma'am?" exclaimed my
> attendant in the greatest possible amazement. "How much per cent, sir?" said I,
> repeating my question. His reply was lost on my ear, save, "Madam, at any rate
> do not trifle with my feelings." "At any rate, did you say? Then take six per cent;
> that is the easiest to calculate." Suddenly I found myself deserted—why or
> wherefore I was too busy to conjecture. (Ethel Parton, 97)

The sprightly tone of this early essay is indicative of the talent for satire
and invention that would later win her many devoted readers.

Marriage and Tragedy

It is safe to assume that Sara Willis did not view her essay on
mathematics as the beginning of a career as a writer. When she left the
Hartford Female Seminary, it was to go home to Boston to await the next
stage in her life: marriage. Yet while she was courted by a number of
young men, she continued to hone her literary skills by writing pieces for
her father's publication *The Youth's Companion*, then in its early years of
circulation. No doubt Nathaniel Willis welcomed the assistance of his
talented daughter, but clearly she was merely marking time until the
right suitor came her way. As Florence Adams states, "Deacon Willis'
advanced ideas of education did not include careers for his daughters—
marriage was the consecrated lot of women" (4). Indeed, as Fanny Fern
later commented in the *New York Ledger*, she had returned home to "learn
the 'Lost Arts' of bread-making and button-hole stitching."[17]
    The right suitor turned out to be Charles Harrington Eldredge, the
son of a Boston physician, Hezekiah Eldredge, who had served as
president of the Massachusetts Medical Society. Charles Eldredge held a
position as a cashier at the Merchant's Bank of Boston and had a
promising career in banking before him. The couple, by all accounts very
much in love, were married on 4 May 1837. Charles Eldredge's salary was
sufficient to support a family, and the next few years of Sara's life were
occupied happily enough with her duties as wife and mother. The couple

had three daughters during these years: Mary, born in 1838; Grace Harrington, 1841; and Ellen Willis, 1844.[18] Proximity to the families of both Sara and Charles allowed for frequent visiting, and Sara settled into the life of a young Boston matron which her culture had dictated for her.

A series of unexpected losses, beginning in 1844, shattered this domestic peace and forced Sara Willis Eldredge along the road to becoming Fanny Fern. In February 1844, her youngest sister, Ellen, died in childbirth, and shortly thereafter her mother, Hannah, also died. In the following two years, tragedy struck even closer to home: in March 1845, Sara's eldest daughter died of brain fever at age seven; in October 1846, Charles Eldredge died of typhoid fever. The grief that Sara experienced especially over the deaths of her daughter and husband informs the descriptions of similar events in her novel *Ruth Hall*, and her experience with losing a young child lay behind the fervor with which she would later describe such losses in her *Fern Leaves* collections. Two passages from columns in the *New York Ledger* dated 10 years apart show the persistence of her sense of loss. In 1859, Fanny Fern wrote, "I love to think that heaven is full of little children. I have one there; and though I shed many bitter tears when she went, oh how I have blessed God since that he took her."[19] And in 1869, three years before her own death and 24 years after Mary's, she expressed much the same sentiment: "It is long years since I shed a tear over mine . . . the shining lock, the little shoes. I can take them out of their wrappings in my hand and smile to think that I am so far on my way that I shall soon see my little one face to face."[20] Sara's religious belief, even if not as orthodox as Deacon Willis would have wished, offered her consolation in times of trouble.

For the next few years, financial difficulties proved to be even thornier than emotional ones. Though Charles Eldredge had been a young man with a promising future, he left his wife very little at his death. He had been engaged in a business enterprise that had resulted in a lawsuit, and when the case was decided against him, his creditors bore away much of what would have been his young widow's inheritance. In the midnineteenth century, a widow had essentially two ways available to support herself and her children: she could remarry, or she could rely on her family and/or her husband's family for financial support. With neither the inclination nor any immediate prospects for marriage, Sara Eldredge turned to her parents and her in-laws, but to little avail. For reasons that can only be speculated about at this point, both sets of parents (Deacon Willis had remarried by this time) were reluctant to provide more than a pittance for the support of Sara and her two daughters. Nathaniel

Willis, like many other men of his time, seems to have believed that once a daughter married the father no longer should be responsible for her financially; Charles Eldredge's parents apparently felt that if Sara had managed more economically during her marriage she would not be in such terrible straits (in *Ruth Hall*, Ruth's mother-in-law is depicted as opposing the marriage in the first place). It seems likely, too, that the independent spirit that was characteristic of Sara Willis would have prevented her from overtly throwing herself on the mercy of either family.

Having been educated but not prepared—either practically or psychologically—for a career, Sara earned small amounts of money from odd jobs deemed "proper" for a woman in her circumstances: sewing, addressing envelopes, selling flowers. At one point she passed the examination necessary to qualify her to teach in the Boston public schools, but actually to get a teaching position required the influence of friends and relatives, so this job did not materialize. This period in Sara's life is detailed in the autobiographical *Ruth Hall* with all the pathos of the struggle for existence; but in the novel Fanny Fern also records the frequently humorous eccentricities of the people inhabiting the cheap rooming house in which Ruth and her daughters live. Sara's powers of observation retained from her experience of struggle and poverty the comic and ironic elements that had earlier characterized her writing and that would flourish in the years ahead.

For Deacon Willis, marriage still seemed the best way out of Sara's financial difficulties, and thus he urged upon her a marriage to Samuel P. Farrington, a Boston merchant and a widower who, like Sara, had two young daughters. The union was clearly, at least on Sara's part, a marriage of convenience, and it soon proved to be a mistake. Although Sara had been candid with Farrington about her lack of deep feeling for him, he was intensely jealous of her, accusing her of infidelity and encouraging his children to spy on her activities. In January 1851, just two years after her marriage to Farrington, Sara took the desperate step of moving out of their home and taking a room at the Marlboro Hotel in Boston, having contacted a law firm to begin divorce proceedings. Her action allowed Farrington to charge her with desertion—a charge that would form the basis of his own divorce proceedings two years later. In addition to angering Farrington, Sara's leaving her husband also alienated her further from her father and the Eldredges, who considered her ungrateful and unworthy of their financial assistance.

The author of *The Life and Beauties of Fanny Fern*, in his effort to denigrate the subject of his "biography," is far more charitable to Samuel Farrington than were other observers of the marriage. He describes Farrington as "a man of energy and upright character" who was "well qualified to sympathize with the young widow" because of his previous experience as a husband and father. He presents the couple's disillusion-ment with the union as mutual: "Fanny learned to her sorrow that all husbands are not equally fond and indulgent; and the bridegroom discovered that Mrs. F. No. 2 wasn't the exact counterpart of Mrs. F. No. 1." The next part of the text wavers between faulting first Sara and then Farrington for the ultimate breakup of the marriage. Moulton first concentrates on Farrington's shock at discovering the difference between his first and second wives: "The contrast was, in fact, so vast and amazing, that it seemed to require solitude and quiet, to consider it in all its bearings. Accordingly, Mr. Farrington resorted to travel and a change of scene; journeyed westward; and has not since been seen on the down-east slope of the continent," (Moulton, 29). Farrington, presented at this point as a man bewildered by the personality of his new wife, is next cast in the role of the villain as, from the safe distance of Chicago, he "legally knocked down his wife with the hammer of divorce," and Sara is described as "once more a widow" (Moulton, 30).

Moulton's ambivalence about the causes of the Farrington divorce, which became final on 7 September 1853, may be due to the fact that Sara subsequently suppressed this episode in her life. Ishbel Ross, in *Ladies of the Press*, concurs with Moulton's assessment of Sara as the deserted wife, despite the fact that Sara moved out first, and states that when Farrington "bolted to Chicago," he "did not even leave his first name behind."[21] And her granddaughter Ethel, writing for *The New Yorker* in 1936, refers to James Parton as her grandmother's second husband, thus omitting the marriage to Farrington from Sara's history.[22] Sara's daughter Ellen seems to have regarded the suppression of the marriage as a personal responsibility. In a letter written in 1899, re-sponding to an inquiry about her mother's marital history, Ellen phrases her response carefully: "Relying upon your promise of secrecy, which I know as a gentleman you will keep, I will answer your first question—My mother *did* marry again in Boston a few years after my father's death . . . his name is immaterial as you will not mention him or the marriage either in person or on paper." (Kelly, 266). It is not surprising, then, that Fanny Fern makes no reference to her second marriage in *Ruth Hall*, which in all other ways is a faithful record of her life to that point. However, the experience is reflected in the marriage and divorce of Gertrude in her second novel, *Rose Clark*. As Mary Kelley writes, "As if she could not avoid it, Parton/Fern appeared to be forever caught in double, if delayed, exposure" (266).

"No happy woman ever writes"

Toward the end of *Ruth Hall*, Ruth's daughter Nettie asks her, "when I get to be a woman shall I write books, Mamma?" "God forbid," Ruth responds, "no happy woman ever writes" (175). Ruth thus locates the motivation for a woman writing in economic hardship. Economic necessity was certainly Sara Willis's motivation following her divorce from Samuel Farrington, despite Moulton's protestations to the contrary in *The Life and Beauties of Fanny Fern*. Moulton writes that Fanny moved from the Marlboro Hotel to "quiet but pleasant lodgings in another quarter of the city" (29). Not only does Moulton maintain that she was not writing because of "starving necessity" when she began submitting columns to his *True Flag*; he refers to her as being "handsomely paid" by his newspaper for her weekly efforts and asserts that "she was at this time living in a style of luxury and elegance which would have reflected no discredit upon any lady of fashion" (44–46). In fact, in order to earn $6 a week, she was writing between five and 10 columns per week for the *Olive Branch* and the *True Flag*. In contrast to Moulton's description of these years is that of her third husband, James Parton, in his *Memorial Volume*: "a situation inexpressibly forlorn and miserable—dependence in a third-rate boarding house. . . . They were years of wretchedness, which left deep traces upon her nature, never wholly obliterated" (49). Reflecting upon his wife's lack of preparation to make her own way in the world, Parton pauses in the midst of his biographical sketch to comment on the tendency of affluent families to unfit their daughters for self-sufficiency:

It is only in the United States, and in a few circles of Great Britain, perhaps, that educated women can get to the age of thirty-six, *wholly* unversed in that useful, unromantic lore which we call knowledge of the world. During their childhood they are caressed, indulged, and forbidden to go into the kitchen. They do not learn the prices of things. They have not the smallest conception of the difficulty of maintaining human lives. Their burden is borne by others, and they accept the good things of this life as the flowers receive the sunshine and the dew, without any knowledge of the stress and toil by which these things are won; and, during a prosperous and happy married life, all the ugly places in the pathway

are often hidden from them by their husband's forethought and tenderness.
They know nothing of his business. They know nothing of any business. The
consequence is that, if they are suddenly bereft of that strong arm and that
providing mind, they are likely to be, for a time, bewildered, distracted, and
helpless. (50)

Whatever were the precise circumstances of Sara Willis's life during
the period in which she was becoming Fanny Fern (and James Parton is
surely not a fully objective source), her later newspaper columns clearly
conveyed that she understood the conditions of urban poverty during the
midnineteenth century. It is also clear that for a time in the early 1850s
she was unable to support both of her young daughters and was forced to
send her older daughter, Grace, to live with Charles Eldredge's parents.
Even Moulton acknowledges that "her eldest daughter [was] residing
with her grandfather Eldredge" (45), an arrangement that Sara Willis
would not have willingly sought and one that is described in *Ruth Hall* as
particularly dismal for both mother and child.

Sara Willis was certainly not the first woman to turn to the pen for
economic survival. As both Helen Papashvilly and Ann D. Wood have
noted, women writers of the midnineteenth century were seldom motivated simply by a desire for self-expression or an attempt to make their
mark on literary history. In *All the Happy Endings*, Papashvilly comments
that many of these women were widows, often, as in the case of Sara
Willis, with small children to support.[23] Ann Wood points to the fact
that the economic impetus made women's relationship to their writing
quite complex: "On the one hand, economic necessity was a better excuse
for writing than a sheer burning unladylike desire for self-expression. On
the other hand, it was . . . taboo for the lady writers to be what
Hawthorne realized they were: shrewd competitors in the literary
market . . . Various women writers took different ways of repressing
awareness, in their readers and in themselves, of this facet of their literary
activity."[24] Some writers, such as Harriet Beecher Stowe and Susan
Warner, claimed that God inspired—even commanded—their work;
others, such as Sarah Josepha Hale, were open about the economic
"emergency" that compelled a woman to "sacrifice . . . female sensi-
tiveness" and make herself "conspicuous" (Wood, 10).

Such anxiety about adopting the position of public writer was well-
founded. Hawthorne was not alone in denouncing the "scribbling
women"; a backlash against women writers was given voice in both
England and America. In 1850, for example, English critic and novelist

George Henry Lewes issued "A Gentle Hint to Writing Women" in which he asks, "Does it never strike these delightful creatures that their little fingers were made to be kissed and not to be inked?" Protection of women's "little fingers," however, is the least of Lewes's concerns, which turn far more on self-interest: "Does it never occur to them that they are doing us a serious injury, and that we need 'protection'? Woman's proper sphere of activity is elsewhere. Are there no husbands, lovers, brothers, friends to coddle and console? Are there no stockings to darn, no purses to make, no braces to embroider?" But Lewes is not merely concerned that women fulfill their domestic duties; like Hawthorne, he feared the competition of women writers: "*My* idea of a perfect woman is of one who can write but won't; who knows all that authors know and a great deal more; who can appreciate my genius and not spoil my market."[25]

As the public *persona* of Sara Willis, Fanny Fern did not claim that her work was inspired by God, nor did she apologize for emergency conditions that forced her to take up the pen. The closest she comes to justifying the writing of *Ruth Hall* in her preface to the novel is to write that she hopes the book will "fan into a flame, in some tired heart, the fading embers of hope, well-nigh extinguished by wintry fortune and summer friends" (3). And unlike the central character of her novel, Fanny Fern exhorted women to write as a means of self-expression—including the expression of anger and frustration. One of the essays in her 1868 volume, *Folly As It Flies*, claims women's freedom to write and encourages women to do so as a counter to the monotony of household drudgery. She does not necessarily urge women to seek publication, but instead to use writing as a form of therapy, "a safe outlet for thoughts and feelings."

Anticipating Betty Friedan's *The Feminine Mystique* by nearly 100 years, Fanny Fern refers to the many letters she has received from women and the talks she has had with them as evidence of a deep vein of dissatisfaction: "It is not *safe* for women of 1868 to shut down so much that cries out for sympathy and expression, because life is such a maelstrom of business or folly, or both, that those to whom they have bound themselves, body and soul, recognize only the needs of the former." Such writing, Fern continues, even if in the private form of a diary, can constitute a form of revenge if it is later read by the unresponsive husband or father, who will feel "amazement and remorse" at the sorrow and anger recorded therein. Even if women do not write for the "*world's* eye," they should do it "to lift [themselves] out the dead-level of [their] lives."[26]

Fanny Fern's own writing for the world's eye in the *Olive Branch* and the *True Flag*, both Boston papers, was immediately popular, although it took a while for adequate financial remuneration to follow. Indeed, in July 1851, her first published column, "The Model Minister," earned her only fifty cents from *The Mother's Assistant* and was reprinted in a number of Boston papers in the next few days. In the absence of copyright laws, newspapers were free to copy work from each others' pages, and authors received no additional money for these multiple publications.

One solution to Sara Willis's dilemma would seem to have been within her own family: her brother N. P. Willis was editor of the New York *Home Journal*, and might have been expected to help a talented sister in need. However, when she sent him some of her writing, he returned it with a dismissive letter. N. P. Willis's biographer, Henry A. Beers, later suggested that the editor of the *Home Journal* disliked his sister's "noisy, rattling style,"[27] but it seems likely that he also felt reluctant to enter into a business arrangement with his divorced sister. Whatever the reason, his refusal earned Fanny Fern's unflattering portrait of him as "Apollo Hyacinth" in one of her newspaper columns and in *Ruth Hall*.

For the next two years, Fanny Fern wrote regularly for the *True Flag* and the *Olive Branch*, earning barely enough to survive, but the absence of copyright laws had a positive side: her readership and her popularity extended beyond the readers of these two papers, bringing her to the attention of J. C. Derby, a publisher in Auburn, New York. Derby proposed publishing a collection of Fanny Fern columns—an offer that proved to be the turning point in the author's fortunes. Derby offered her the choice of a lump-sum payment[28] or royalties of ten cents per copy; fortunately, she chose the latter option, because within a year *Fern Leaves from Fanny's Port-Folio*, as the volume was titled, sold nearly 100,000 copies in the United States and Great Britain.

The year 1853 was a time of great change in Fanny Fern's life. In May, she signed the contract with Derby; in September, her divorce from Samuel Farrington became final. Between these two events she moved from Boston to New York, ultimately severing her ties with the Boston papers—an action that led to threats of lawsuits and finally to Moulton's vindictive "biography." The move to New York was prompted largely by an offer from Oliver Dyer, publisher of the *Musical World and Times*, doubling her Boston salary to write exclusively for his paper. With the royalties from *Fern Leaves*, she bought a house on Oxford Street in Brooklyn, leaving her days of boardinghouses and financial anxiety behind.

Family and Fame

When Sara Willis moved to New York, she was accompanied by her
younger daughter, Ellen; Grace, now 12 years old, was still living with
Charles Eldredge's mother. Although Sara was by now fully capable of
supporting both of her children, reuniting her family was made difficult
by the conditions of the will of Dr. Eldredge, who had recently died. He
divided his property between his two granddaughters, but stipulated
that Grace continue to live with Mrs. Eldredge until the latter's death.
Sara was understandably infuriated by this final attempt to separate her
daughter from her, and she returned briefly to Boston to straighten out
the matter. As she remarked at the time, her daughter's "heart is knit to
mine more strongly than children's ordinarily are by sympathy in trial
and sorrow. I shall feel unsettled until I get her with me."[29]

The family unit was completed, by traditional standards, with Sara's
marriage to James Parton on 5 January 1856. Parton had been familiar
with Fanny Fern's work since her earliest columns in the Boston papers.
At that time he was working for N. P. Willis's *Home Journal* as, in his own
words, "assistant-at-all-work," and he became an early admirer. "Finding these Fern Leaves afloat in the papers, and having no suspicion that
the author was in any way related to my chief, I used to clip them
diligently" (*MV*, 54). Parton's championing of the work of Fanny Fern
led to a falling out between him and N. P. Willis, and by the time he met
Fanny Fern in 1853, the two men no longer worked together. At the time
of their marriage, Sara Willis was 44 and James Parton was 33; ahead of
him lay a long and distinguished career as a biographer: from the 1850s
through the 1880s he published biographies of, among others, Aaron
Burr, Benjamin Franklin, Andrew Jackson, Horace Greeley, and Thomas
Jefferson. More shrewd than when she entered into her first two marriages, Sara had her third husband sign a prenuptial agreement stipulat-
ing that her property and the proceeds of her writing belonged solely to
her and her children.

Such property and proceeds were, by the time of her marriage to
Parton, considerable. In September 1853 she contracted with J. C. Derby
for two more books, one a second collection of her Fern Leaves columns
and the other a book for children titled *Little Ferns for Fanny's Little
Friends*. By the summer of 1854, combined sales of her three books had
reached 180,000 copies. On the eve of the tumultuous publicity that
attended the publication of *Ruth Hall*, Fanny Fern was already a well-

known and controversial literary figure. While some critics were already taking her to task for being "irreverent" and "masculine," there could be no doubt about her popularity with readers, as favorable reviewers were quick to recognize. The author of the "Literary Notice" in the 24 December 1854 issue of the New York *Atlas*, for example, thought her popularity well-deserved: "Probably no authoress of the present day has succeeded in enlisting so much popular favor on her side as the really clever and talented authoress of these volumes (*Fern Leaves from Fanny's Port-Folio* and *Little Ferns for Fanny's Little Friends*). She seems to have struck out an entirely new and original path for herself, and risen, at one bold flight, high in the ranks of the most distinguished women of the day."

Reviews such as this one were undoubtedly influential in the sales of Fanny Fern's books, but more important were the unusually flamboyant advertising schemes launched in connection with her novel *Ruth Hall* and her contract to write for the *New York Ledger*. In February 1854, she signed a contract with Mason Brothers publishers to write a "novel or tale," and agreed to suspend all other literary activity until the manuscript was completed. Having stopped writing for the *Musical World and Times* to start contributing a column to the Philadelphia-based *Saturday Evening Post* in November 1853, she ceased her *Post* column as well to devote herself to her novel. Mason Brothers not only promised Fanny Fern fifteen cents royalties on each copy sold, but in November 1854, the publishers mounted a massive advertising campaign for *Ruth Hall*, which was released the following month. Had Mason Brothers known in advance of the storm of controversy that would attend the publication of both *Ruth Hall* and *The Life and Beauties of Fanny Fern*, they might have decided that a more modest campaign would be sufficient.

Hardly had the furor over *Ruth Hall* and its author died down when Fanny Fern contracted to write a weekly column for the *New York Ledger* in 1855—a relationship that continued until her death in 1872. Robert Bonner had recently undertaken to transform a newspaper for businessmen, *The Merchants' Ledger and Statistical Review*, into a major family newspaper. Bonner's strategy was to pay well-known authors handsomely for writing for his paper and at the same time to price the paper low enough that virtually all citizens could afford to buy it. As Florence Adams stated, "The poor could afford to buy it and the less poor could not afford to miss it" (13). In addition to Fanny Fern, Bonner paid large sums to Tennyson, Longfellow, Whittier, Dickens, Edward Everett, Horace Greeley, and Lydia Sigourney. But it was Fanny Fern who, at

$100 per week, became the highest-paid newspaper columnist of the period. Rather than bemoaning the fact that she had driven such a hard bargain, Bonner saw yet another opportunity for publicity and announced her salary to his readers.

Although no single volume of essays was as popular as the initial *Fern Leaves*, Fanny Fern continued to publish such collections until the year of her death. *Fern Leaves*, Second Series (1854), was followed by *Fresh Leaves* (1857), *Folly As It Flies* (1868), *Ginger-Snaps* (1870), and *Caper-Sauce* (1872). As the titles of the later collections suggest, her tone became increasingly satiric and "irreverent" as time went on. Following *Ruth Hall*, she devoted most of her energy and talent to her essays for the New York *Ledger*; a second novel, *Rose Clark*, lacks the fire and the inventiveness of *Ruth Hall*, suggesting that Fanny Fern's primary skills lay in social commentary, rather than fiction. Mason Brothers also published two additional books, which were for children: *The Play-Day Book* (1857) and *The New Story Book for Children* (1864).

In 1859, Sara Willis Parton and her husband sold their house in Brooklyn and moved to a brownstone at 303 East Eighteenth Street in Manhattan, where they lived until her death. By 1863, this household on Stuyvesant Square was also home to Sara's granddaughter Ethel. Her daughter Grace had married Mortimer Thomson in 1861, and died less than two years later, shortly after the birth of her first child. Nicknamed Effie, the child quickly became the center of the Parton's attention and affection. Rather than sending her to school, James Parton educated her at home in his study; similarly, instead of having a servant oversee her activities, Sara and James took their granddaughter for walks and rides. Even though, as Sara wrote to Grace Greenwood, "to carry out such a plan has involved a sacrifice of much literary work, or its unsatisfactory incompleteness," she did not begrudge the time spent: "I am not and never shall be sorry."[30] Having missed part of Grace's childhood, Sara took particular delight in that of Grace's daughter, who assumed the last name of her grandmother when she became an adult.

Ethel Parton's reminiscences of the 10 years that she lived in the Parton household, published in *The New Yorker* in 1936, provide a picture of gracious living among the intellectual elite of Manhattan in the 1860s. She recalls Robert Bonner's stable of fine racehorses, the Hamilton Fish estate near the Parton house, trips to bookstores, and visits with family friends such as William Cullen Bryant, Bret Harte, and Horace Greeley. The family had servants, sometimes freed slaves but more often young Irish girls (who were often illiterate). Of her grandmother, Ethel remarks, "she was a columnist before columnists were heard of; her book 'Fern Leaves' and its successors were best-sellers before that term was invented" (32). She also reports that Fanny Fern thought through her columns while brushing her hair or taking long walks through the city, a practice corroborated by James Parton in his *Memorial Volume*, in which he reports that once she had determined her topic, the writing itself was a matter of a few minutes—usually just before her deadline: "It was never possible to induce her to write a day before her article was due at the printing-office. She would often put it off till the last moment, and then, taking her pen in hand, would finish the piece in about the time that I, for example, would usually employ in getting started" (56). This method of composition contributes to the immediate, conversational style of many of her articles.

This public *persona* that readers came to know so well continued to mask the private life of Sara Willis Parton. Despite the fact that the progressive, humanitarian views expressed in print by Fanny Fern were those of Sara as well, she seldom became active in social movements, and given her caustic comments about the frivolities of fashionable society, she preferred the company of other writers during summers spent at Newport. Sara Parton did, however, sometimes actively pursue the rights of women—a frequent topic in her newspaper columns. One notable example is her involvement in the formation of Sorosis, a press club for women. Having discovered that the Press Club did not intend to invite women to a dinner party that it was giving for Charles Dickens in 1868, Sara and several other women journalists formed their own organization, which barred men from participation in its activities.

During the last six years of her life, Sara Willis Parton battled cancer, a fact that Fanny Fern was determined to keep from her readers. She never missed writing her weekly columns, even when, in the last months of her life, she was forced to dictate them to her husband, having lost the use of her right arm. James Parton reports that when it was clear that she was dying, she insisted on writing a note to Robert Bonner saying that "the omission [of her column] was *for that week only*" (81). So completely had she become Fanny Fern that her own continued existence seemed dependent upon presenting that public self to readers of the *Ledger*.

Following Sara Parton's death on 10 October 1872, her granddaughter Ethel was sent to live with Sara's daughter Ellen, whom James Parton later married. On 2 November, the editorial page of the *Ledger* was edged in black as Bonner's tribute to her, and a few weeks after her death a letter to the editor testified to the extent of her fame and influence:

Mr. Bonner: I saw yesterday as I was standing in the Union Depot in Cleveland, Ohio, a magnificent Pullman car. The name on it surrounded by a golden wreath was—FANNY FERN—and, as I looked at it, the many helpful words she had written came to my mind and I said to myself—"Fanny Fern is a name that will be remembered as long as memory lasts."

A Freight Conductor

Chapter Two

Sentiment and Satire: *Fern Leaves*

The Rise of the Columnist

The twentieth-century newspaper, with its clear distinction between the objective reporting of news and the opinions expressed on editorial pages, is the product of a long evolution in which columns such as those of Fanny Fern played an important role in the midnineteenth century. Although the editorial pages and the choice of which stories to give prominence may still cause newspapers to be regarded as "liberal" or "conservative," their political biases are quite muted when compared to the overt partisanship of America's earliest newspapers. Nathaniel Willis's creation of the *Eastern Argus* as a paper that would espouse Whig views in opposition to the Federalist stance of the *Portland Gazette* in the early nineteenth century was typical of the period. In the absence of other media that could inform and influence the electorate, newspapers were often clearly identified with specific political interests. In addition to serving political ends, nineteenth-century newspapers also served as outlets for fiction, poetry, and essays on the arts and culture—a function still performed in some small towns and rural areas. The few poems of Emily Dickinson that were published during her lifetime appeared in the *Springfield Republican*, a newspaper published in Springfield, Massachusetts, and many lesser-known authors looked to the newspaper as one of the few available forums for their work.

The newspaper column that develops a clear *persona* and perspective—such as contemporary columns by Art Buchwald and Ellen Goodman—emerged as a hybrid of the political and creative impulses. As partisan control of newspapers began to decline after 1830, a number of editor-writers put their stamp on their newspapers by championing various causes and commenting on a wide range of social and cultural issues. Editors such as Horace Greeley and Samuel Bowles expressed concerns about American culture that rose above specific party platforms to concern themselves with ethics and morality. In an era of intense struggle to define a national identity, such writers were as likely to lecture their readers on the state of the arts as to espouse the abolitionist cause. The fact that such editor-writers were expressing personal, individual views rather than reflecting the stances of parties or groups justified their addressing a variety of topics without claiming a particular expertise in all areas; they wrote, as Fanny Fern was later to do, as educated, alert citizens possessed of the right to express their opinions in print. Twentieth-century columnist Westbrook Pegler would later call into question the credentials of writers who displayed such a catholicity of interests. Pegler defined a columnist as one who "knows all the answers off-hand and can settle great affairs with absolute finality three or even six days a week." Living in an era of greater specialization than was the nineteenth century, Pegler expressed concern about the authority that print could lend to the nonexpert: "What is it that you would like to be told about by your favorite myriad-minded commentator? Economics, pig prevention, the Constitution, the law, politics, war, history, labor, the C. I. O. and the A. F. of L., housing, Naziism, Communism, inflation, agriculture or phrenology? Name me something we can't tell you all about with absolute irrefutable authority and no two, perhaps, in agreement on any single point."[1] Despite Pegler's reservations, the tradition of the "myriad-minded" columnist has flourished in American newspapers since the midnineteenth century.

Robert Bonner, publisher of the *New York Ledger*, was instrumental in the transition from the editor-writer, such as Greeley and Bowles, to the commentator invited to contribute regular, signed columns to a newspaper. Born in Ireland, Bonner emigrated to the United States in 1839, at age 15. Following a five-year apprenticeship to a printer in Hartford, Connecticut, Bonner moved to New York to work as a printer for the *New York Evening Mirror*. His skills as a printer soon attracted the attention of the owner of the *Merchants' Ledger*, who hired Bonner to work for that paper. By the time he was 26, Bonner had bought the *Merchants' Ledger* from its previous owner and set out to transform it into a general-interest paper that would have wide appeal to readers. The commercial emphasis of the paper was gradually replaced by a focus on literature for family reading, beginning with serialized stories pirated from London papers. By 1855, the name of the paper had become simply the *Ledger*; it was a weekly combination of magazine and newspaper that featured popular literature as well as news and financial reports. Such weekly papers were intended to appeal to a mass audience, and therefore included features that would attract readers with different interests; in addition to serialized fiction, each issue might include a fashion column, an agricultural column, and a humor section, along with selected news stories. Bonner's *Ledger* advertised itself as devoted to "Choice Literature, Romance, The News, Commerce," and in this sense was little different from other such periodicals. What distinguished Bonner's paper was the inclusion of the signed weekly column—and hence the development of the columnist as highly-paid celebrity.[2]

Although Robert Bonner gambled on the success of his newspaper in some ways, he took few chances in selecting the authors whom he invited to contribute fiction, poetry, and columns to the *Ledger*. Most were household words: Charles Dickens, Henry Wadsworth Longfellow, William Cullen Bryant, Alfred Lord Tennyson. Nor did he ignore the fact that the majority of readers of the literary weeklies were women. In addition to Fanny Fern, Bonner engaged the services of Harriet Beecher Stowe, Mary Virginia Terhune, E. D. E. N. Southworth, and Lydia Sigourney. By 1855, when Fanny Fern began writing regularly for the *Ledger*, her first two volumes of *Fern Leaves* had been published to resounding success, and the controversy about her novel *Ruth Hall* had only increased her prominence. Nor was Fanny Fern taking any great risk by committing herself to write exclusively for Bonner's paper: not only was she handsomely rewarded financially, but she was also able to continue writing the pithy, conversational columns that suited both her temperament and her readers.

Fern Leaves

As Fanny Fern notes in the Preface to the first volume of *Fern Leaves*, published in 1853, many of the selections in the volume were written originally for the Boston *True Flag* and *Olive Branch* and the New York *Musical World and Times*, whereas others were written specifically for the volume. The opening paragraphs of the Preface seem to be a combination of the conventional author's apology for the book and Fanny Fern's genuine surprise that she is to have a book in print: "I never had the slightest intention of writing a book. Had such a thought entered my mind, I should not long have entertained it. It would have seemed presumptuous. What! *I*, Fanny Fern, write a book? I never could have believed it possible. How, then, came the book to be written? some one may ask. Well, that's just what puzzles me. I can only answer in the dialect of the immortal 'Topsy,' 'I 'spect it growed!' And, such as it is, it must go forth. . . ." The author goes on to say that she wishes the book were "worthier of your regard. But I can only offer you a few 'Fern leaves' gathered at random, . . . which I little thought ever to *press* for your keeping" (*Leaves*, n. p.). The play on the word *press* is characteristic of the kind of word play that Fanny Fern was increasingly fond of using.

In characterizing what she terms the "articles" in *Fern Leaves*, Fanny Fern makes several suggestive comments: "Some of the articles are sad, some are gay; each is independent of all the others, and the work is consequently disconnected and fragmentary; but, if the reader will imagine me peeping over his shoulder, quite happy should he pay me the impromptu compliment of a smile or a tear, it is possible we may come to a good understanding by the time the book shall have been perused." Of the 115 short selections in this first volume of *Fern Leaves*, more than one-half are more apt to evoke tears than smiles; more than a dozen of the sketches have as their subject the death of infants or small children, and others deal with neglected children, young widows, and the consolations of religion. Slightly more than midway through the collection, such topics give way to pointedly satiric sketches of pompous, self-indulgent, hypocritical people. Despite the mixture of tones, and despite Fern's description of her book as "disconnected," the *persona* that emerges is consistent in her values: a deep belief in family, motherhood, love, and charity, and an equally deep distrust of cant, selfishness, and the pretensions of genteel culture. Drawing upon her own experience and perceptions, Fanny Fern clearly intended her reader to "come to a good understanding" of these values and priorities.

At least two dozen of the essays and stories in *Fern Leaves*—including those that deal with the deaths of small children—are in some sense autobiographical, and a number of these seem to be preliminary sketches for her novel *Ruth Hall*. In "Summer Days; or, the Young Wife's Affliction," the idyllic marriage of a young couple comes to an end with the death of the husband from a fever. Not only does this recall the death of Charles Eldredge, but the author also emphasizes the young widow's ensuing poverty: "the necessary disposal of every article of luxury . . . her removal to plain lodgings . . . her untiring efforts to seek an honorable, independent support" (*Leaves*, 46). In "Dark Days," a young widow named Janie confronts an unfeeling world as she tries to support herself and her child by working as a seamstress; when the child dies, she recalls the words of her dying husband; "who will care for you, Janie, when I am dead?" (*Leaves*, 185). The story "Thorns for the Rose" parallels in part the account of Ruth Hall being forced to send one of her daughters to live with her husband's parents for a time. In the novel, this story has a happy ending when the child is restored to her mother, but in the *Fern Leaves* sketch the child dies and the mother is driven mad by grief.

Not all of the autobiographical sketches in *Fern Leaves* end tragically. Some show the young widow using her talent as a writer, like Ruth Hall, to triumph over both adversity and individual adversaries. The most extended treatment of this theme is contained in "The Widow's Trials." In this story the young widow is again named Janie; she has one child—a son—to support, and immediately thinks of writing as a way to do so. The person from whom she initially seeks assistance in this endeavor is an amalgam of three characters that were to figure in *Ruth Hall*: Ruth's brother, the self-interested writer and publisher Apollo Hyacinth; Ruth's sanctimonious father; and her father-in-law. Uncle John, this composite figure in "The Widow's Trials," is the editor of a highly successful newspaper named *The Morning Star* and is a hypocritical Christian. Pathos and satire are mingled in this sketch as the widow's plight is juxtaposed to scathing portraits of Uncle John such as the following: "Uncle John was a rigid sectarian, of the bluest school of divinity; enjoyed an immense reputation for sanctity, than which nothing was dearer to him, save the contents of his pocket-book. . . . He pitied the poor, as every good Christian should; but he never allowed them to put their hands in his pocket;—that was a territory over which the church had no control,—it belonged entirely to the other side of the fence" (*Leaves*, 18–19). Uncle John thus combines the parsimoniousness of Ruth Hall/Sara Willis's father and father-in-law with the lack of charity of Apollo/N. P. Willis. When Janie, in "The Widow's Trials," approaches her uncle about writing for his newspaper, he rejects her: "Can't afford to pay contributors, especially new beginners. Don't think you have any talent that way, either. Better to take in sewing, or something" (*Leaves*, 20). His remarks prefigure Ruth Hall's brother's denial of her talent for writing and his cavalier suggestion that she find another means of supporting herself. Yet, like Ruth Hall, Janie succeeds as a writer without the assistance of her relatives, whereupon Uncle John is quick to claim their kinship: "he took a great deal of pains to let people know that this new literary light was *his niece*" (*Leaves*, 23).

Several other *Fern Leaves* sketches foreshadow characters and incidents in *Ruth Hall*. In "Self-Conquest," a young bride endures the criticism of her mother-in-law, who accuses her of being a spendthrift, criticizes her housekeeping skills, and resents the time she spends with her own mother. Like Mrs. Hall, the mother-in-law in "Self-Conquest" seems to resent having to share her son with anyone, and she makes the young woman's life miserable. Fortunately, the husband is sensitive to his wife's plight and buys a house in the country where the couple can live in peace. "A Page from a Woman's Heart" is the story of a young woman who has been deserted by her husband and receives no assistance from her wealthy father as she attempts to support herself and her child by writing translations. Trying to maintain her dignity and self-sufficiency, she rejects an offer of help from a young man who admires her; but when she faints in the street from hunger and fatigue, the young man's father decides to adopt her, telling her father, "She is my daughter from his day, sir, and may God forgive your avarice!" (*Leaves*, 310).

Still other sketches in this first collection of *Fern Leaves* include clear autobiographical elements that are not so clearly incorporated into *Ruth Hall*. Sara Willis's ambivalent feelings about her own religious upbringing surface in several of the selections. In "The Prophet's Chamber," for example, she recalls the frequent visits to her father's house in Boston (changed in the story to her grandfather's house) by members of the clergy. Calling the house "to all intents and purposes, a ministerial tavern;—lacking the sign" (*Leaves*, 214), Fanny Fern writes of the warm hospitality extended to these visitors by Deacon Willis and his wife, and recalls her particular joy at the visits of the Reverend Edward Payson, from Portland, Maine, to whom Sara Willis owed her middle name. Called "Mr. Temple" in this sketch, but identified by James Parton as the Reverend Payson (*MV*, 28), he is described as a kind, gentle man who was especially fond of children and told them Bible stories in his "low and musical voice" (*Leaves*, 216). Such attentiveness by this clergyman seems to have inspired the young to model behavior, at least temporarily: "I used to think that if I could always live with dear Mr. Temple I should never be a naughty little girl again in my life—never! never!" (*Leaves*, 217). But the high spirits that led to childhood "naughtiness" also produced sketches such as "A Fern Soliloquy," in which she satirizes the churchgoing behavior of the "Misses Pecksniff," whose uniformity of dress and demeanor suggests a hypocritical piety: "[W]ith their six pink silk bonnets, and six rosettes on corresponding sides; with their six sky blue shawls, crossed over their six unappropriated hearts, six pair of brimstone kid gloves, clutching six Village Hymn Books, folded in six pocket-handkerchiefs trimmed with sham cotton lace; six muslin collars, embracing their six virgin jugulars, fastened with six gold crosses all of a size! It's perfectly annihilating!" (*Leaves*, 375). Fanny Fern's mention of the Misses Pecksniffs' "unappropriated hearts" and "virgin jugulars" suggests that their appearance in church has less to do with religious devotion than with attracting husbands.

Also growing out of the experience of Sara Willis are Fanny Fern's sketches that deal with the woman as professional writer. These sketches, taken together, provide insight into several aspects of the situation of the woman writer in the midnineteenth century, including the attitudes of men toward what was termed the "bluestocking," and writing as financial salvation. In both "The Practical Blue-Stocking" and "A Chapter on Literary Women," Fern reflects the widespread assumption that the "scribbling woman" was ill-suited to be a wife and mother, her literary activity making her impractical and unfeminine. The most direct statement of this assumption occurs in "The Practical Blue-Stocking," in which a young man is reluctant to visit a friend who has recently married a woman writer. As he tells his uncle: "I understand he has the misfortune to have a blue-stocking for a wife, and whenever I have thought of going there, a vision with inky fingers, frowzled hair, rumpled dress, and slip-shod heels has come between me and my old friend—not to mention thoughts of a disorderly house, smoky puddings, and dirty-faced children. Defend me from a wife who spends her time dabbing in ink, and writing for the papers. I'll lay a wager James has n't a shirt with a button on it, or a pair of stockings that is not full of holes" (*Leaves*, 100).

Finally persuaded to visit his friend James, Harry finds that his fears are unfounded: James's wife is attractive and well-groomed, and she serves them a wonderful meal. When Harry confesses his former suspicions about literary women to James, he is further informed that James's wife had begun writing in secret at a time when the family finances were in jeopardy, and her success had saved them from ruin. The message is clear: the literary woman is acceptable if she is discreet about her activities and if she does not neglect her domestic responsibilities in favor of her writing. This same theme is central to "A Chapter on Literary Women," in which Colonel Van Zandt seeks a wife, but does not want a "literary woman": "I should desire my wife's thoughts and feelings to centre in me,—to be content in the little kingdom where I reign supreme,—to have the capacity to appreciate me, but not brilliancy enough to outshine me" (*Leaves*, 176). Because of her use of a pseudonym, the Colonel is unaware that the woman he marries is a successful writer, but he is not dismayed when her identity is revealed to him, because she has proven herself to be attentive to him and to their home. At the conclusion of the story, the Colonel sums up prevailing opinion when he announces that "a woman may be literary, and yet feminine and lovable; content to find her greatest happiness in the charmed circle of Home" (*Leaves*, 179).

The idea that a woman could be accepted as a writer only if she maintained the proper standards of femininity is also elaborated in the sketch titled "Our Hatty." A young woman who is regarded as unattractive and unintelligent by her family comes under the loving influence of a family friend—an unmarried woman who encourages her latent talents as a writer. When she is later revealed to her family as the author of a book of poems, Hatty wants their love more than their admiration of her talent: "O, what is Fame to a woman? Like the 'apples of the Dead Sea,' fair to the sight, ashes to the touch!" (*Leaves*, 39). Home and the love of family, not fame, were supposed to be woman's rewards. As Susan Coultrap-McQuin states in *Doing Literary Business*, "Being woman was the primary fact and being womanly the major glory, according to the proponents of True Womanhood. . . . being a True Woman was a vocation in itself, more distinguished than any other."[3] So deeply was this concept ingrained in women of the period that Fanny Fern's contemporary Grace Greenwood, who obviously admired the boldness of her writing, felt constrained to emphasize Fern's adherence to standards of female behavior: "whatever masks of manly independence, pride, or mocking mischief Fanny Fern may put on, she is, at the core of her nature, 'pure womanly'" (Greenwood, 84).

Part of the task of the free-lance writer, male or female, was of course to interest editors of periodicals in their work. Given Sara Willis's initial difficulties in placing her work with editors, it is not surprising that two of the satiric portraits in *Fern Leaves* are of newspaper editors, emphasizing the luxuries to which they are treated and the general ease of their lives. In "Editors," Fanny Fern describes editors as spending their days smoking cigars, receiving visitors, and exchanging political and social gossip. The men described here, like those in "Everybody's Vacation Except Editors," are the recipients of free passes to plays and other entertainments, free books for reviewing, and "a slice of wedding-cake every time a couple makes fools of themselves" (*Leaves*, 367). Yet in another sketch, Fanny Fern takes the side of the editor whose work day is interrupted by a boring visitor named "Mr. Leisure," who uses the newspaper's stationery to write a letter, smokes the editor's cigars, and criticizes his newspaper. Given the fact that satiric sketches of other "types" appear in *Fern Leaves*, this piece seems more a generic portrait of "Mr. Leisure" than a defense of editors, and Fanny Fern had not yet found the editor—specifically, Robert Bonner—who could change her impressions of the profession to positive ones.

The type of column that Fanny Fern had developed by the time the first volume of *Fern Leaves* was published in 1853 was one that would vary little during her career: a brief story or monologue that illustrates a moral, ethical, or social point. Whether sentimental or satiric, the pieces begin without preamble and establish immediately the tone the column will have. A piece about a homeless child, for example, begins in short, matter-of-fact sentences—"It is only a little pauper. Never mind her" (*Leaves*, 105)—establishing the cold attitude of the public toward those in need. In contrast, a satiric sketch titled "Bachelor Housekeeping" begins with crisp, vivid phrasing that quickly establishes Fanny Fern's attitude: "I think I see him! Ragged dressing-gown; beard two days old; depressed dickey; scowling face; out at elbows, out of sorts, and—out of 'toast!' " (*Leaves*, 324). The sketches in the first two volumes of *Fern Leaves* display an impressive range of voices and attitudes, as Fanny Fern responded to whatever issue claimed her attention, from the amusing plight of the helpless bachelor to the real tragedy of neglected children. In her later collections of columns, the voice is more consistent, as Sara Willis's *persona* becomes more secure in a stance of moral outrage, and she largely abandons the use of pathos to make her point. But Fanny Fern's role remained that of gadfly rather than reformer; she seldom proposed solutions to the problems she identified, except by implication. In "Fanny Fern: Our Grandmothers' Mentor," Elizabeth Bancroft Schlesinger comments on the columnist's limitations as a social reformer: "Her interest in social problems was emotional and romantic. Often sorrowing over the tribulations of the poor, she never troubled her head over the causes of their pitiful lives, nor did she offer any suggestions for improvement. . . . Likewise her concern for the unhappy inmates of a prison reached no further than her inkpot. She frequently chided women about their treatment of servants, but withheld any criticism of employers who allowed thousands of women to work under wretched conditions."[4] While it is true that Fanny Fern did not offer programs for social reform in her columns, it is important to keep in mind that despite strong movements for female suffrage and the abolition of slavery, the 1850s was not an era of widespread social reform such as that which would characterize the end of the nineteenth century. Nor was Sara Willis in any sense trained as a social scientist; her role as columnist was to entertain and to some extent enlighten her readers. Indeed, it is remarkable that, especially in her writing for the *New York Ledger*, she was able to identify such a great number of social issues, from the frivolity and artificiality of women's fashions to the failure of conventional religion to minister to the real needs of people.

By far the majority of the selections in the first volume of *Fern Leaves* deal with human relationships, especially those in the family setting: parents and children, husbands and wives, grandparents and stepmothers. Like most of those raised in America's genteel culture in the early nineteenth century, Sara Willis had been taught that the family was a sacred institution, and Fanny Fern holds the happy nuclear family in high esteem. This is particularly evident in her many depictions of the sorrow attending the disruption of the family unit, such as through the death of a spouse or a child. It is also clear that most of the responsibility for family unity and harmony falls on the woman. In "How Husbands May Rule," for example, a young wife gives up a close friend whom her husband dislikes. The issue is clearly that of the husband wishing to maintain control over his wife, because when the wife protests that her friend is "lady-like, refined, intellectual, and fascinating," her husband responds that it is these very qualities he is afraid will influence "one so yielding and impulsive as yourself" (*Leaves*, 116). In "How Woman Loves," the wife's sacrifice is far greater: when her husband is sent to prison for embezzlement, she not only remains loyal to him, but also withholds from him the news of the death of their son, so as not to increase his unhappiness. At the end of the story, a stranger remarks that her face reminds him of "a Madonna,—so pensive, sweet and touching" (*Leaves*, 156).

Although at this point in her career Fanny Fern to some extent approved of such female self-sacrifice, she had no sympathy for the cruelty with which men could treat women. Such behavior is always linked, as in "How Husbands May Rule," to a masculine need for control. In both "Mary Lee" and "Edith May," the husband's obsessive jealousy leads to the wife's destruction. In a story horrifying in its simplicity, Mary Lee's husband's unfounded jealousy prompts him to commit her to an asylum, where she pines away and dies. The husband in "Edith May" is more calculating. Edith has married the "ossified old bachelor," Mr. Jones, following a quarrel with her true love. Although Edith is a faithful wife to Jones, he tests her by leaving on a business trip and arranging for word of his death by drowning to be sent to her. After a suitable period of mourning, Edith and her young lover are reunited, whereupon Jones appears to claim his wife, saying, "I happen to be manager here, young man!" (*Leaves*, 113). Edith dies within a week, and her lover goes insane. Sometimes such tyrannical men are eventually made to feel remorse for their behavior—but only after members of their families have died. In "The Passionate Father," a man who bullies his wife and his young son learns to control his temper only after his son dies. "Grandfather Glen" tells the story of a wealthy man who has banished his daughter when she married a man who was not his choice. Now living in poverty with her consumptive husband and six-year-old son, the daughter sends her father, on Thanksgiving Day, a plea for help, which he ignores. In desperation, she next sends her son in hopes of softening the heart of Grandfather Glen; the strategy works, but she and her husband die before help arrives.

Such sketches, with their innocent, imperiled children and long-suffering wives and mothers, are undeniably melodramatic, a fact which was doubtless part of their appeal to the midnineteenth-century reader. But they also reflect certain cultural realities: the economic dependence of women, the vulnerability of children to now-preventable diseases, and the sin-and-redemption theme promulgated by conventional religion. Another reality of nineteenth-century culture was the role of women as stepmothers—not, as is the case today, as a result of divorce, but as the result of the mother's death, frequently in childbirth. At the time that Fanny Fern wrote the sketches collected in this first volume of *Fern Leaves*, she had not yet experienced the role of stepmother in her brief marriage to Samuel Farrington, but in three of the sketches she demonstrates her understanding of the difficulties inherent in the position. In two of these—"The Lost and the Living" and "The Step-Mother"—Fanny Fern shows women overcoming their stepchildren's resistance to them through loving persistence, but the third takes a satiric approach to the situation, suggesting that no amount of self-sacrifice on the stepmother's part can make everyone happy. "The Model Step-Mother," which is one of several descriptions of "models" filling various roles in the volume, delineates in a series of clauses the efforts of an unnamed, generalized stepmother to please everyone. She "gratifies every childish desire, how injurious soever, or unreasonable, and yet maintains the most perfect government; . . . looks as sweet as a June morning, when she finds them in the kitchen, lifting the covers off pots and kettles." Yet, "after wearing herself to a skeleton trying to please everybody, has the satisfaction of hearing herself called 'a cruel, hard-hearted step-mother'" (*Leaves*, 301–2).

Despite Fanny Fern's sympathy with the difficulties of women's lives, she was not at this point in her career an outspoken proponent of women's rights. Having begun her career as a professional writer just a few years after the 1848 Seneca Falls Woman's Rights Convention, Fanny Fern was well-aware of the controversy surrounding such outspoken women and was reluctant at this point to identify herself with them. As Elizabeth Schlesinger describes the situation, "Females on public platforms were damned before opening their mouths. Many prominent women who worked unceasingly for better education and wider opportunities for their sex were unwilling to fight for their political rights. Their arguments buttressed the sheltered wives and daughters who balked at the idea of voting. Many feminine writers strove hard to dissociate themselves from their unladylike belligerent sisters" (513). The most direct statements regarding women's rights in *Fern Leaves from Fanny's Port-Folio* occur in "A Little Bunker Hill," which is a response to a statement by an unidentified author urging that "rights are rights, and, if not granted, should be demanded." Fanny Fern first notes that she hopes "no female sister will be such a novice as to suppose [the statement] refers to any but masculine rights," and goes on to call the issue of women's rights "debatable ground," and "a vexed question." Conscious of reactions against what Schlesinger terms "unladylike belligerent sisters," Fern asserts that "granted we had 'rights,' the more we 'demand,' the more we shan't get them," and she ends her brief essay by advising, "Make your reins of silk, keep out of sight, and drive where you like!" (*Leaves*, 346–47). The same advice—and indeed the same imagery—characterizes "The Weaker Vessel," in which Fanny Fern asserts that "what can't be had by force, must be won by stratagem." Women's strength lies in getting what they want without appearing to do so: "It is only very fresh ones, Monsieur, who keep the reins in sight" (*Leaves*, 338).

At the same time that she encouraged subterfuge instead of overt action, however, Fanny Fern made clear that the institutions—chief among them marriage—that were supposed to protect women and make them happy frequently failed to do so. In addition to the cruel, jealous husbands depicted in "Mary Lee" and "Edith May," she satirizes in several sketches the notion that marriage is the fulfillment of every woman's dream. In "The Tear of a Wife," she adopts the stance of someone scolding women who dare to reveal that they are not perfectly happy in their marriages: "You miserable little whimperer! what have you to cry for? A-i-n-t y-o-u m-a-r-r-i-e-d? Isn't that the *summum bonum*,—the height of feminine ambition? You can't get beyond that! It is the jumping-off place! You've arriv!—got to the end of your journey!

Stage puts up there! You have nothing to do but retire on your laurels, and spend the rest of your life endeavoring to be thankful that you are Mrs. John Smith!" (*Leaves*, 324–25). "Aunt Hetty on Matrimony" takes a similarly jaundiced view of marriage, although in a straightforward rather than parodic way. Fern's *persona* warns a group of young women that "Love is a farce; matrimony is a humbug; husbands are domestic Napoleons, Neroes, Alexanders,—sighing for other hearts to conquer, after they are sure of yours" (*Leaves*, 377). Aunt Hetty characterizes husbands as penny-pinching, inattentive, and useless as parents, but ends by acknowledging the power of cultural mythology: "I'll warrant every one of you will try it the first chance you get; for, somehow, there's a sort of bewitchment about it" (*Leaves*, 379).

Shadows and Sunbeams

The irreverent tone associated with Aunt Hetty dominates the second volume of *Fern Leaves*, published in 1854. Reprinted under the title *Shadows and Sunbeams* by the John W. Lovell Company of New York, this collection of columns seems—as well it might—more self-assured, its author more experienced and cosmopolitan. Fewer of these sketches are autobiographical and melodramatic; more of them address social issues, from religious hypocrisy to prison conditions, with many satiric looks at marriage and domestic life. Fanny Fern's deep concern for the welfare of children is still evident, and death is described in mournful tones, but her eye ranges widely over human concerns and situations most often in a mood of detachment or even skepticism.

Several techniques and approaches that appear in the first volume of *Fern Leaves* are used more frequently in *Fern Leaves*, Second Series. These became established trademarks of the "Fern Leaves" columns—of Fanny Fern's distinctive style—and some of them prefigure the characteristics of twentieth-century newspaper and magazine columnists. One of these devices is the column as a response to a statement made by another writer—frequently an anonymous statement. The quoted statement, set as an epigraph, serves as a springboard for Fanny Fern's views on the same subject, enabling her to enter into a kind of public debate on matters of manners or morality. Many of these columns respond to pieces of advice or conventional maxims. "Sunshine and Young Mothers," for example, is a rebuttal to the conventional wisdom that women are at their most contented as wives and mothers; the quoted statement concludes, "If you would take a peep at sunshine, look in the face of a young mother," to which Fanny Fern retorts, "They are worn to fiddle strings before they are twenty-five!" Despite her reverence for the mother–child relationship, she declares that marriage is a *"one-sided* partnership," with the wife responsible for the care of both husband and children, making her old before her time (*SS*, 144–45). In "Mrs. Weasel's Husband," Fanny Fern's *persona*, Mr. Weasel, takes issue with the old saw, "A woman, a dog, and a walnut tree, / The more they are beaten the better they be." Married to a woman who rules the household and attends women's rights meetings, Mr. Weasel does not dare confront his wife, let alone beat her: "I'd as lief face a loaded cannon!" (*SS*, 187).

Fanny Fern's columns are frequently responses to contemporary news items, and prefigure a similar technique used by such writers as E. B. White and Dorothy Parker in the early twentieth century—notably in *The New Yorker.* "A Model Husband," for example, is a response to the news that the husband of a woman who has eloped with another man has given her $100 to help with her expenses. Fanny writes that if she were the wife, she would return to such a magnanimous husband and do her best to keep him happy. In more than one of these columns, Fanny Fern extends the dialogic nature of the informal newspaper piece by responding to an item in which she has herself been quoted. Such is the case in "Who Would be the Last Man." An anonymous writer quotes Fanny Fern as having stated that "If there were but one woman in the world, the men would have a terrible time," and asks her to comment on what would happen were there only one man left—whereupon she remarks that, for her, "the limited supply would not increase the value of the article" (*SS*, 95). Several of these response columns serve as reminders of the close literary ties between the United States and England in the midnineteenth century, when the absence of international copyright laws facilitated the reprinting of British publications in this country. Items in the British humor periodical *Punch* serve as provocations for several "Fern Leaves," including one in which she takes issue with "Mr. Punch's" assertion that whereas men will admit that they are wrong, women will confess only to being "mistaken" (*SS*, 257–58). She is in complete agreement, however, with William Thackeray's remark in *Household Tyrants* that "A husband may kill a wife gradually, and be no more questioned than the grand seignor who drowns a slave at midnight." In a remarkably insightful response, Fanny Fern comments on the kind of emotional wife abuse that is difficult to prove, "So the only way we can get along, is to allow them to scratch our faces, and then run to the police court, and show 'his Honor' that Mr. Caudle can '*make his mark*'" (*Leaves*, 245).

Wife abuse is the subject of other selections in *Fern Leaves*, Second Series, most forcefully in "Our Nelly," a mournful tale of a lovely, gentle young girl whose spirit—and subsequently life—is destroyed by a mean husband. Fanny Fern's narrator in this sketch is explicit about the lack of legal protection for such abused women in terms that sound remarkably contemporary: "Ah! There is no law to protect women from negative abuse!—no mention made in the statute book (which *men frame for themselves*), of the constant dropping of daily discomforts which wear the loving heart away—no allusion to looks or words that are like poisoned arrows to the sinking spirit. No! if she can show no mark of brutal fingers on her delicate flesh, he has fulfilled his legal promise to the letter—to love, honor and cherish her. *Out* on such a mockery of justice!" (*SS*, 216). More minor forms of unfair treatment of women by men include women's economic dependence. In "Women and Money," Fanny Fern responds with indignation to the quoted pronouncement that "A wife shouldn't ask her husband for money at meal-times." In Fanny's opinion, women who have shown themselves to be capable of managing money sensibly should not have to beg their husbands for money at *any* time. The annoyances of marriage are detailed in "How Is It?"—especially a husband's thoughtlessness and inattentiveness: "Think of Mr. Snip's lips being hermetically sealed, day after day, except to ask you 'if the coal was out, or if his coat was mended'" (*SS*, 118–19).

Although by far the majority of Fanny Fern's columns in this volume are brief and topical, some are longer, more reflective essays that record the panorama and variety of urban life in the manner of the "Talk of the Town" section of *The New Yorker*. As immigration and industrialization began to create distinct urban centers in the Northeast, there was much to remark in the contrast between rich and poor, the simple and the pretentious, the transient life of hotels and boardinghouses and the permanence of great houses. The society that Fanny Fern describes in these essays is one still in transition from frontier to settled metropolis; ladies' skirts get muddy in unpaved streets, and there are no social services to see to the needs of homeless children, but the "cult of gentility" affects the buying habits of a growing middle class that yearns to be fashionable. The three-part "City Scenes and City Life" records impressions of street vendors, urban architecture, and earnest people going to work while "the fashionables" are still asleep—scenes, as she writes, worthy of the engraver William Hogarth. Stereotypes typical of the period abound in these sketches: boardinghouses have "slip-shod Irish servants" (*SS*, 322), and a Spanish-speaking immigrant dies before a priest can hear his last confession. In addition to using national types, Fanny Fern also notes several emerging urban types, such as the "New York business men, with their hands thrust moodily into their coat pockets, their eyes buttoned fixedly down to the sidewalk, and 'the almighty dollar' written legibly all over them" (*SS*, 317).

Although Sara Willis was a city-dweller all her life—first in Boston and then in New York—Fanny Fern many times expresses a preference for country life, with its nostalgically imagined purity, virtue, and human caring. The two worlds already seemed so irretrievably different by the early 1850s that one accustomed to life in either city or country found it difficult to be transplanted. In a number of sketches, "Jonathans" from the country are duped by urban con artists, and Fanny Fern anticipated by 100 years the plight of the suburban commuter: in "Uncle Ben's Attack of Spring Fever, and How He Got Cured," Uncle Ben finds it difficult to give up the conveniences of urban life when he moves his family to the country for the summer. Contrasting city Sundays to country Sundays, Fanny Fern emphasizes the commercialism and frivolity of the former and the peace and serenity of the latter; and in "The Fashionable Preacher," she describes a fashionably dressed congregation ministered to with sophisticated rhetoric, but lacking true piety and conviction: "Oh, there's intellect there—there's poetry there—there's genius there; but I remember Gethsemane—I forget not Calvary!" (*SS*, 231). Worst of all is to be ill in the city, where even your neighbors do not know you, as opposed to experiencing illness in the country, where, "unchilled by selfishness, unshrivelled by avarice, human hearts throb warmly" (*SS*, 272). Fanny Fern's attitude toward the artificiality and pretention that she associates with urban life is best summarized by her essay titled "Best Things," in which she argues against owning useless finery—"a carpet too fine to tread upon, books to dainty to handle, sofas that but mock your weary limbs" (*SS*, 161).

As in the first volume of *Fern Leaves*, Fanny Fern remarks in this second volume on the situation of the woman writer. Several of the sketches here describe the hostility of editors and critics to female authors. The sources of such male scorn for the female writer seem to be a need for power and control, and an unwillingness to separate the author's work from her personal life. In the "Soliloquy of Mr. Broadbrim," a critic feels that a woman whose work has gotten good reviews might become too "conceited," and sees it as his responsibility to "take the wind out of her sails." Sanctimoniously, he decides that for the "welfare . . . of her soul" he must "annihilate her" in his review (*SS*, 63). Although Fanny Fern could not have anticipated that the publication of her novel *Ruth Hall* would be followed by Moulton's antagonistic "biography," *The Life and Beauties of Fanny Fern*, she describes, in "Critics," one who would "lash a poor, but self-reliant wretch, who had presumed to climb to the topmost round of Fame's ladder, without *his* royal permission or assistance, and in despite of his repeated attempts to discourage her" (*SS*, 87–88)—a statement that seems to echo perfectly Moulton's attitude.

In addition to the resentment of female writers by those who felt that their territory had been usurped, women faced the dilemma of public versus private. In spite of the fact that writing was a relatively acceptable career for a woman by the 1850s, in part because she could write while remaining in the domestic setting, the duties of her role as mother and homemaker often interfered with her profession—a circumstance that Virginia Woolf was later to term "The Angel in the House"—the person whose time is always considered interruptible. Although little evidence suggests that Sara Willis/Fanny Fern was often a victim of the "Angel in the House" syndrome—certainly not during her marriage to James Parton—she had no difficulty imagining a woman having to juggle her two responsibilities. In "Mrs. Adolphus Smith Sporting the 'Blue Stocking,'" Fanny Fern depicts a woman trying to finish a newspaper column while interrupted repeatedly by her husband, children, and servant, until she is finally driven to comment, "It's no use for a married woman to cultivate her intellect" (*SS*, 102). The selection in *Fern Leaves*, Second Series, that most directly predicts the controversy that would greet the publication of *Ruth Hall* is "Have We Any Men Among Us?", in which she writes, "Time was, when a lady could decline writing for a newspaper [*as Fanny Fern had refused to continue to write for Moulton's True Flag*] without subjecting herself to paragraphic attacks from the editor, invading the sanctity of her private life" (*SS*, 181). Yet if Fanny Fern had not written *Ruth Hall*, and thereby invited such "invasion," her reputation might not have been revived more than a century later, and the "Fern Leaves" columns might have been forgotten.

Chapter Three

Fame and Controversy: *Ruth Hall*

The "Women's" Novel

In order to understand the significance of Fanny Fern's first novel, *Ruth Hall*, in both its own historical moment and as part of the reevaluation of women's literary history, one must consider the literary culture of which it was a part—specifically, the tradition of what has been variously called the "domestic" novel, the "sentimental" novel, and the "women's" novel of the nineteenth century. Since 1956, with Helen Waite Papashvily's *All the Happy Endings*—but especially since the 1970s—scholars have devoted considerable attention to this body of fiction, revealing the complexity of its authorship, readership, and thematic content. Papashvily emphasized the sameness of these novels in setting, theme, and intent: "The center of interest was the home although that edifice might range from one of Mrs. E. D. E. N. Southworth's noble English castles to the tastefully adorned wigwam of Malaeska in Mrs. Ann Stephen's book of the same name. The common woman was always glorified, her every thought, action, gesture, chance word fraught with esoteric meaning and far-reaching influence; her daily routine of cooking, washing, baking, nursing, scrubbing imbued with dramatic significance; her petty trials and small joys magnified to heroic proportions"(xvi). By focusing on the home as the domain in which women had their greatest power and influence, such novels both reflected and reinforced the "cult of domesticity" that made home and family life the source of moral strength for the culture as a whole. The Victorian ideal of the middle class in the midst of the nineteenth century moved the locus of power from "patriarchal authority" to "domestic affection," as the "public" and the "private" spheres became increasingly separate, with women expected to exert influence only in the latter.

Yet at the same time that these novels stressed the confined nature of women's sphere of influence, they in several ways underscored women's strength and even attempted to subvert the values of the patriarchal culture. Papashvily no doubt claimed too much when she asserted that these books were "handbooks" of "feminine revolt" that "encouraged a pattern of feminine behavior so quietly ruthless, so subtly vicious that by comparison the ladies [at the Seneca Falls Convention] appear angels of innocence" (xvii). Papashvily based her contention on the frequent portraits in these novels of men who abandoned or otherwise injured women, pointing to the fact that the authors of these novels had frequently had such experiences, resulting in what she termed "a chronic grievance" (xvi). While it is true that Fanny Fern turned her grievances against several men in her family into scathing portraits in *Ruth Hall*, the typical plot of the domestic or sentimental novel posits marriage as the solution for women's problems—constituting the "happy endings" of Papashvily's title. Yet the fact of abandonment (including that occurring through death, as in *Ruth Hall*) frequently leaves the heroine on her own for a time, forced by circumstances to be independent, to make decisions. In *Woman's Fiction*, Nina Baym describes the paradigmatic plot: "In essence, it is the story of a young girl who is deprived of the supports she had rightly or wrongly depended on to sustain her throughout life and is faced with the necessity of winning her own way in the world. . . . [H]er story exemplifies the difficult but successful negotiation of the undifferentiated child through the trials of adolescence into the individuation of sound adulthood. The happy marriages with which most . . . of this fiction concludes are symbols of successful accomplishment of the required task and resolutions of the basic problems raised in the story."[1]

In *The Adventurous Muse*, William C. Spengemann distinguishes between the "poetics of domesticity" and the "poetics of adventure," proposing that the domestic novel, which "illustrate[s] and inculcate[s] the predominantly social and familial values of stable perpetuity, resignation, prudence, modest ambition, acceptance, conformity, and reconciliation," arose in eighteenth-century England "in reaction to the very sorts of social disruption and ideological upheaval which the discovery of America had done so much to foment and which the poetics of adventure were devised to validate."[2] The novel of adventure, then, arose as a manifestation of the spirit of movement and travel—*away* from home rather than *toward* it—and was particularly suited to American authors. What Spengemann thus suggests as a *national* division had become a *gender* division in American fiction by the midnineteenth century, with Huck Finn "lighting out for the territory" while female protagonists sought the fixed environment of home. In the domestic novel, Spengemann notes, "travel and adventure—all metaphors of *movement*, in fact—suggest error or misfortune" (71). Having developed the self-control and moral purity that makes her marriageable, the heroine of such novels is rewarded by acquiring a setting in which to exert her moral influence. Female strength is thus defined as self-denial: denial of any impulse that would lead to autonomy rather than connectedness, independence rather than familial duty.

Two of the most popular authors of American domestic fiction, which Baym identifies historically as beginning in the 1820s with the work of Catharine Sedgwick and ending about 1870, with the work of Augusta Evans, were E. D. E. N. Southworth and Susan Warner. Southworth's *The Curse of Clifton* (1852) and *The Hidden Hand* (1859) and Warner's *The Wide, Wide World* (1850) contain many elements that characterize the genre. In Southworth's novels, the heroine shows enormous skill and intelligence as a young woman; in *The Curse of Clifton*, Catherine Kavanagh competently runs two plantations, and in *The Hidden Hand*, Capitola fends for herself in an urban setting, even dressing in men's clothing and fighting a duel. But all of these accomplishments are merely a prelude to marriage, after which the women's moral virtue becomes ascendent over her intelligence and resourcefulness. Catherine Kavanagh even manages the moral reform of her husband, a former reprobate who comes to realize that she is "better" than he is. In Warner's fiction, moral virtue is derived directly from religious orthodoxy; her heroines endure numerous trials with their faith in God's goodness unshaken. The separation of mother and child is a common element in nineteenth-century women's novels and Ellen, in *The Wide, Wide World*, is sent by her invalid mother to live with a grim relative in the country. The strength-under-adversity that Ellen develops during this and a later exile to even more distant relatives in Scotland prepares her for eventual marriage to a young minister.

Although Baym several times in *Woman's Fiction* expresses exasperation at these novelists' adherence to what has been termed the "marriage plot" (of *The Hidden Hand*, for example, she writes, "one would wish that, in her repeated depictions of strong and superior women, Southworth had left an occasional heroine unmarried, as sign that glamor might adhere to a single woman" [26]), women writers had powerful reasons to use formulaic plots: namely, critics and the reading public. Numerous commentators on the literary scene in the midnineteenth century pronounced on the assumed talents and limitations of women writers in ways that restricted them to the expectations of the domestic novel. For one thing, women were perceived to be good at describing what they had actually observed, but deficient in imagination. British journalist R. H. Hutton, in 1858, attempted to account for what he termed the "main deficiency" of "feminine genius": "It can observe, it can recombine, it can delineate, but it cannot trust itself further; it cannot leave the world of characteristic traits and expressive manner, so as to imagine and paint successfully the distinguishable, but not so easily distinguished, world out of which these characteristics grow. Women's fancy deals directly with *expression*, with the actual visible effects of mental and moral qualities, and seems unequal to go apart, as it were, with their conception, and work it out firmly in fields of experience somewhat different from those from which they have directly gathered it."[3] Such definitions of women's limited talents in novel-writing—which virtually restricted them to writing about the domestic realm they by and large inhabited—also had the effect of ensuring that they would not produce "great" literature. As another English critic asserted in 1860: "The female novelist who keeps strictly to the region within which she acquires her knowledge may never produce a fiction of the highest order, but she will be in the right path to produce the best fiction of the class in which she is most likely to excel."[4] It was such prescriptions of the areas that women's fiction should deal with that the American humorous writer Marietta Holley made fun of a decade later in the preface to her first book. With mock humility, Holley writes of her lack of qualifications for authorship: "I cant write a book, I don't know no underground dungeons, I haint acquainted with no haunted houses, I never seen a hero suspended over a abyss by his galluses, I never beheld a heroine swoon away, I never see a Injun tommy hawked, nor a ghost; I never had any of these advantages; I cant write a book."[5]

Readers as well as critics and reviewers put pressure on authors to write within certain traditions. In *Ruth Hall*, Fanny Fern reproduces several letters that Ruth's newspaper columns elicit from readers, showing the personal relationship that may develop through print. That such correspondence could help to shape a writer's work is demonstrated clearly in Susan S. Williams's article "Widening the World: Susan Warner, Her Readers, and the Assumption of Authorship." Like Ruth Hall (and Fanny Fern), Susan Warner began writing because of economic necessity; unlike her, Warner never achieved a level of prosperity that could free her from pleasing her readers. Williams's examination of the original manuscript of the *The Wide, Wide World* and correspondence

from Warner's readers allows her to argue convincingly that Warner
consciously tailored her themes and language for an audience accustomed
to a certain level of purity and piety in female heroines. The published
version of *The Wide, Wide World* contains pious passages not present in
the manuscript; further, a concluding chapter not retained in the published version describes a level of worldly luxury at odds with the
ultimate piety of the heroine. After this first novel had established Susan
Warner's reputation as a sentimental novelist, readers were quick to
point out any lapses from the standard it established. Williams notes, for
example, that "one woman scolded Susan for using the words 'deuced,'
'cursed,' and 'devil' in *Stephen, M. D.* (1883)."[6]

The terms used to characterize the genre in which Warner and so
many other women wrote are worth analysis, because they reveal the
circumstances which both produced this body of fiction and caused it to
be relegated to the footnotes of American literary history by the end of
the nineteenth century. The term *sentimental novel* is today the most
pejorative of these labels, although its origins are merely descriptive: by
dealing with the realm of human relationships—parents and children,
husbands and wives—this fiction necessarily focused on human emotion
and sentiment more than on physical or ideological conflict. While many
of these novels are undeniably sentimental in the commonly understood
sense of that term, with scenes and language designed to elicit tears from
sympathetic readers, the authors were in large part following the convention of a narrative tradition in which male authors participated as
well. Such "sentimentality" can be found in the work of several canon-
ized nineteenth-century writers such as Poe, Hawthorne, and Cooper.
The less pejorative term *domestic novel* arises from the values of home and
family that these novels espouse and for which their authors were
assumed to have a special affinity. Yet as Corinne Dale has argued, to
identify "domestic" writing only with women writers is to create a false
and simplistic distinction. Dale cites the domestic imagery of such
Puritan poetry as Edward Taylor's "Huswifery," the male domestic
community of Melville's *Moby-Dick*, and the traditions of plantation and
frontier fiction as evidence that male authors have valued and accentu-
ated the domestic setting and their place within it. "By insisting," Dale
writes, "that domestic literature is women's literature or that women's
literature is domestic literature, many call for a separate but equal
position, not true integration."[7] Nina Baym chooses the more neutral
term *woman's fiction*, which suggests that the readers as well as the writers
of these narratives were primarily, though not exclusively, women.

Whatever term is used to designate this popular body of fiction published between 1820 and 1870, the novels arise clearly from cultural ideologies of the period. They stress the home as the locus of moral influence and the woman as central to the maintenance and transmission of values. Marriage is the necessary goal of a woman's life, not as an end in itself, but because it establishes the domestic setting in which she may exert her influence. Heroines may demonstrate enormous ingenuity, strength, and intelligence as adolescents and young women, but the trajectory of their lives is toward home and family rather than toward a public, autonomous existence. While the portrayal of men in some of these novels as unfaithful, selfish, and even brutal may constitute in some cases a subversive protest against patriarchy, it also serves to underscore the contrasting virtue and nurturance assumed to be characteristic of women.

Against the "Marriage Plot"

Ruth Hall, while participating in some of these conventions, charts a different trajectory for its heroine. Rather than ending with marriage, the novel begins with Ruth's marriage to Harry Hall; further, on the eve of her marriage Ruth is not in a rapture of bliss about her new life, but instead has fears about the future. Two of these fears center on her future husband's character and constancy: "[W]ould a harsh word ever fall from lips which now breathed only love? Would the step whose lightest footfall now made the heart leap, ever sound in her ear like a death-knell? As time, with its ceaseless changes, rolled on, would love flee affrighted from the bent form, and silver locks, and faltering footsteps? Was there no talisman to keep him?"[8] Ruth's concerns about being abused or cast aside by her husband prove to be groundless; the marriage, despite considerable interference on the part of Harry's mother, is a happy one. Harry is sensitive to Ruth's anguish over the meddling of her in-laws, and moves her to a house of their own in the country—a circumstance that Fanny Fern also described in the sketch "Self-Conquest," in the first volume of *Fern Leaves*. The less specific anxieties about her future that Ruth experiences before her marriage are, however, realized in the deaths of her firstborn, and, eight years and two more children later, of her husband, Harry.

Thus, in a novel subtitled *A Domestic Tale of the Present Time*, the heroine spends less that one-third of the story in a traditional domestic setting; the independent struggle for survival that normally precedes the heroine's marriage here takes place following that marriage. Also, Ruth's endeavors outside the domestic sphere are not intended to prepare her morally to be a wife, but instead to set her on the path to a professional career. In this respect, as Joyce W. Warren has pointed out, the plot resembles that of the Horatio Alger genre that would be popular later in the nineteenth century, in which the hero moves from poverty to financial security by virtue of his own talents and persistence.

Ruth's long struggle for financial security begins immediately after Harry's funeral, when Ruth's father and father-in-law both express their reluctance to support Ruth and her two daughters, even though each is a prosperous man. Ruth's mother-in-law, who had always opposed the marriage, announces her intention to take "Harry's" children from Ruth, a scheme at which she partially and temporarily succeeds later in the novel, when Ruth is unable to support both children. With her familial adversaries thus lined up against her, Ruth leaves her sunny cottage and moves with her children to a cheap boardinghouse in the city. She first attempts to earn a living as a seamstress; next she applies to be a primary school teacher, but without someone influential to pull strings for her, she is unable to obtain a position. The scenes describing Ruth's failures, fatigue, and anxieties are written with sentiment and even pathos, but they are interspersed with sprightly, often satiric chapters depicting life in the boardinghouse and on the streets.

By the time Ruth begins her attempt to earn a living as a journalist, she has suffered two additional setbacks. Her brother, Hyacinth, a prosperous magazine editor, has coldly refused to employ her as one of the contributors to his publication, thereby joining the ranks of the family arrayed against her; and her mother-in-law has succeeded in taking Ruth's daughter Katy to live with her, not because of any love or concern for the child, but out of spite. While the loss of her daughter is a severe blow to Ruth, Hyacinth's rejection of her work serves to energize her to succeed as a writer: "I *can* do it, I *feel* it, I *will* do it" (*RH*, 116). This determination to prove her brother wrong marks the turning point for Ruth. Although she is poorly paid at first, Ruth's newspaper columns, written under the pseudonym "Floy," soon attract a substantial readership, in large part due to their spirited nature. Because she and her editor keep the real identity of Floy a secret, many readers assume her to be a man, "because she had the courage to call things by their right names, and the independence to express herself boldly on subjects which to the timid and clique-serving, were tabooed" (*RH*, 133).

Like the Horatio Alger hero, Ruth is assisted by luck as well as by her own skill and determination. Her columns come to the attention of John Walter, publisher of the "Household Messenger" (a thin disguise for Robert Bonner, of the *New York Ledger*); Walter offers Floy a contract to write exclusively for his paper, and soon she is able to achieve financial independence. It is important to note that although Ruth Hall has a male "savior," what he offers her is a job, not his hand in marriage; indeed, Fanny Fern is careful to provide John Walter with a wife in order to preclude that possibility, and the final chapter of the novel includes a visit to Harry Hall's grave, as if to reinforce Ruth's fidelity to her one true love. Also significant is that one day in the same mail Ruth receives two proposals of marriage and a letter from a publisher offering to publish a collection of her columns. She ignores the offers of marriage without comment, but responds immediately to the publisher, demonstrating both shrewd business sense and faith in her own popularity when she chooses to take royalties on the book rather than selling her copyright to it for $800. By the end of the novel, Ruth, with both of her daughters, is preparing to move to another part of the country to pursue her career as a writer. John Walter, described as a "*true* friend," remarks to Ruth that "life has much of harmony yet in store for you" (*RH*, 210-11), and thus concludes the novel on a note of future possibilities rather than closure.

 Ruth Hall consists of 90 short chapters, few of them more than two or three pages long. In their brevity, these chapters resemble Fanny Fern's newspaper columns, and the similarity does not end there. Even though Fanny Fern sustains the narrative flow of the novel, she shifts her angle of vision and her style with each new chapter, which gives the novel the texture of a tapestry in which midnineteenth-century life is presented, if not comprehensively, certainly with a consciousness of variations in social class and degrees of reverence toward middle-class ideologies. Although Fanny Fern employs an omniscient narrative perspective, presenting scenes that Ruth Hall does not directly witness and the thoughts of those other than Ruth, the implied narrative stance is hers—or perhaps one should say that of Fanny Fern—throughout. That is to say, the satiric portraits of Ruth's foppish brother, Hyacinth, and the hypocritical Dr. and Mrs. Hall originate in the values that produce Ruth's anguish at the death of her one daughter and her dedicated struggle to provide for her remaining daughters, Katy and Nettie. As is the case with Fanny Fern's newspaper columns, the tone and style of each short chapter of *Ruth Hall* differs from the one that precedes and follows it.

 The novel's structure as a series of vignettes is described in Fanny

Fern's preface, in which she explains that she has "avoided long introductions and descriptions, and [has] entered unceremoniously and unan-
nounced, into people's houses" (RH, 3). This casual description belies
Fanny Fern's control over the tone and perspective of each chapter.
Recent scholars have seen the language used by the nineteenth-century
woman novelist as the product of conscious selection rather than the
passive assimilation of convention. As Susan Williams has shown, Susan
Warner chose to write with a piety that would appeal to her readers and
ensure her economic survival. The choice of stylistic methods in Ruth
Hall is more complex and reflects Fanny Fern's determination to use the
language of both sentiment and satire for her own purposes. Whereas
Ann D. Wood finds the alternation of sentimental and ironic approaches
in Ruth Hall to be evidence of a struggle between acquiescence to and
rejection of the language of "true womanhood," Susan K. Harris has
proposed that twentieth-century readers have misunderstood the uses to
which nineteenth-century women writers put the language they employed:

Our interpretive conventions have been inadequate for assessing just how
deliberately nineteenth-century women writers were capable of manipulating
the writing conventions of their day. Ruth Hall is an excellent text to.begin
reexamining this question because in it Fern used sentimental imagery and
language patterning as means, first, of disguising her goal to project a woman
who grows into self-definition and verbal power and, second, of bringing the
worldview implicit in the sentimental mode into doubt. In exploiting and
subverting a rhetorical mode not only closely associated with women's writing
but also commonly held to be reflective of women's nature itself, Fern was
actively challenging the prevailing nineteenth-century view of ideal women.[9]

Rather than dismissing the language of sentiment, Harris suggests
that we see it as a set of codes that establishes a character's position within
a hierarchy of virtues. "By associating Ruth with flowers and piety Fern
creates a protagonist her readers will recognize as deeply feminine, a
woman who feels as a woman should feel, and who therefore qualifies as
a heroine the general culture can accept" (113).

In chapter 1 of Ruth Hall, Ruth is associated with moonbeams and
roses; the reader is told that she can blush, and that at boarding school she
was shocked by the mischievousness of her classmates. When Ruth gives
birth to her first child, in chapter 7, Fern emphasizes the sense of
womanly fulfillment that the event represents—"that most blessed of all

hours. Ruth is a *mother!*"—and stresses the "God-commissioned" nature of maternal responsibility and influence (*RH*, 24). Furthermore, Ruth's virtue is tested by the interference of her mother-in-law, who cautions her to read sermons on predestination rather than novels, criticizes her housekeeping, and even objects to the fact that Ruth's hair is naturally curly. Ruth endures these challenges stoically, with "cold bathing and philosophy," managing "self-conquest" rather than complaining to her husband (*RH*, 21). Such forbearance is rewarded by a house of her own several miles from the clutches of her in-laws.

Yet even in the early chapters of the novel, while Fanny Fern establishes Ruth's conventional female virtues, she also suggests the lack of reverence for convention that will increasingly characterize Ruth's perspective. Her mother-in-law's cautions and criticisms, for example, are so exaggerated as to seem ridiculous. Among her suggestions for Ruth's reading is "Seven Reasons why John Rogers, the martyr, must have had *ten* children instead of *nine* (as is *generally* supposed)" (*RH*, 21); not content to advise Ruth not to keep running home to her father, she denies that the married Ruth even has a father anymore. After Ruth's daughter Daisy is born, Mrs. Hall is filled with dire predictions that Ruth will lose her hair and her teeth, and comments that the baby is "quite a plain child" who "don't favor our side of the house at all" (*RH*, 26). The first of the full-blown satiric portraits in *Ruth Hall* occurs in chapter 8. The description of Mrs. Jiff, Ruth's nurse during her convalescence from childbirth, stands in sharp contrast to the rhapsodic tribute to motherhood in the preceding chapter. Mrs. Jiff is a fat, snuff-taking woman who devotes herself to her own pleasures of eating, drinking, gossiping, snooping, and napping rather than caring for Ruth and the baby. Her presence is far more irritating than soothing to the young mother; she has "a wheezy, dilapidated-bellowsy way of breathing . . . which was intensely crucifying to a sick ear," and Ruth is described as the "helpless victim" of this loud, careless woman (*RH*, 25). Even as the behavior of Mrs. Hall and Mrs. Jiff undermines the bliss of motherhood, Fern maintains Ruth's virtuous nature. Instead of protesting about her treatment at the hands of Mrs. Jiff, Ruth "innocently wondered . . . whether there would be any impropriety" in asking the nurse to change her ways (*RH*, 26).

Ruth's silence and submissiveness in this situation is not only evidence of her femininity as an adult woman, but is also traced to its origins in her childhood. Like so many women authors, Fanny Fern emphasizes the early silencing of her central female character. Most of what Ruth remembers about her mother, who died when Ruth was young, is her fear of Ruth's father's emotional tyranny; hearing her husband's footsteps coming home, Ruth's mother admonishes the children to "Hush! Hush! your father is coming" (*RH*, 14). Such silencing—coupled with the disdain with which she is treated by her adored older brother, Hyacinth—causes Ruth to be a lonely, solitary child. But as with other silenced female characters (e.g., Celie in Alice Walker's *The Color Purple* and the narrator in Maxine Hong Kingston's *The Woman Warrior*), language itself eventually proves to be the key to self-definition and autonomy. Even in the first chapter are hints of Ruth's innate facility with the written word. A "fine passage in a poem" would make "her heart thrill" (*RH*, 14), and when she goes to boarding school she excels at writing compositions—a fact that recalls Sara Willis's prizewinning essay on the horrors of learning mathematics when she was a student at Catharine Beecher's school. Hyacinth's later refusal to publish Ruth's writing amounts to an extension of her childhood silencing, which serves as one impetus for her determination to succeed as a writer.

As both Joyce Warren and Susan Harris have pointed out, another motivation for Ruth's determination to seek economic independence through her writing is her observation of two women whose dependence on men emphasizes the problematic nature of such relationships. The stories of Mrs. Skiddy and Mrs. Leon may seem at first glance extraneous to Fanny Fern's narrative of Ruth Hall, but in fact they illustrate the two choices Ruth has at this point, and the vastly different styles in which the stories of these two women are told serves to undercut further the conventional ideals for women's lives. Mrs. Skiddy's is the comic story of the woman who runs a cheap boardinghouse where Ruth and her children live after Harry's death. Tired of her husband's often-articulated desire to seek his fortune in California, Mrs. Skiddy leaves for a time with two of their children, leaving behind an infant for Mr. Skiddy to care for in his own bumbling way. The experience does not cure Mr. Skiddy of his wanderlust, however, and he boards a ship for California, whereupon Mrs. Skiddy prospers with the boardinghouse. When, a year later, he writes to ask his wife for money for the passage home, she contemplates "a purse well filled with her own honest earnings" and utters the single word "N-e-v-e-r!" (*RH*, 109). Mrs. Skiddy represents the woman who has long ago decided to be in charge of her life; as she tells Ruth, "when a woman is married, Mrs. Hall, she must make up her mind either to manage, or to be managed; *I* prefer to manage" (*RH*, 106-7).

In contrast to the lower-class but independent Mrs. Skiddy, Mary Leon, whom Ruth meets at a seaside hotel, has wealth and privilege, but she is a very unhappy woman in a loveless marriage to a man who, though generous to her with his money, is cold and unfeeling. Mr. Leon is described as a man who maintains "under all circumstances the same rigidity of feature, the same immobility of the cold, stony, gray eye, the same studied, stereotyped, conventionalism of manner" (*RH*, 50). Mr. Leon eventually commits Mary to an insane asylum while he goes to Europe, a fact that Ruth discovers shortly after Mary's death in the asylum. A note that Mary has, too late, written to Ruth protests that she is not crazy, and begs Ruth to take her away from the asylum. The pathos of the scene in the asylum, in contrast to the comic elements of Mrs. Skiddy's "managing," subverts the concept of woman's security in marriage; the language of sentiment is attached to woman's defeat, whereas the language of satire is connected to woman's triumph.

Satiric Realism

As Joyce Warren has stated, virtually all of the negative criticism of *Ruth Hall* following its publication in 1854 was directed at the novel's author rather than at the novel itself. The book was termed "abominable," "monstrous," and "overflowing with an unfemininely bitter wrath and spite," and the fact that the negative response was triggered largely by a woman portraying satirically her male relatives is encapsulated in a review in the New Orleans *Crescent City* from which Warren quotes: "As we wish no sister of ours, nor no female relative to show toward us, the ferocity she has displayed toward her nearest relatives we take occasion to censure this book that might initiate such a possibility" (*RH*, xvii). In other words, Fanny Fern had not failed as a novelist, but rather as a daughter and a sister, for not showing the proper respect for her male relatives. Such critical responses overlooked the fact that *Ruth Hall* includes satiric sketches of women—some of them Ruth's relatives—as well as men, and that several men are portrayed quite favorably, even heroically. Rather than making her judgments on the basis of gender or family relationship, Fanny Fern made them according to a set of values in which hypocrisy, greed, and self-interest were to be castigated, and generosity, kindness, and integrity were to be praised—ironically, the same set of values promulgated by the genteel piety that Fanny Fern was supposed to have transgressed.

Ruth's father, Mr. Ellet, and her brother, Hyacinth, are presented from the earliest pages of the novel as self-important and self-serving. When Ruth, attempting to please her brother, takes lunch to him in his room, he confuses her with the servant. For Mr. Ellet, Ruth is more annoyance than daughter, and the moment his wife dies he packs her off to boarding school. These dismissive attitudes continue and deepen as Ruth becomes an adult. When Hyacinth visits Ruth at school, she is thrilled, for "she loved him, poor child, just as well as if he were worth loving," but he responds by criticizing her appearance and insisting that she learn to waltz (*RH*, 16). After Ruth has become a widely published columnist despite Hyacinth's refusal to help her, Hyacinth is presented as a man not only egotistical, but also duplicitous. In a chapter told from the perspective of an editor for Hyacinth's "Irving Magazine" the reader learns that Hyacinth has taken credit publicly for an article that the editor, Horace Gates, has written. Hyacinth also, in the same chapter, instructs Gates by letter not to use any of "Floy's" columns in his magazine, because it would "mortify [him] exceedingly" if it were known that she is his sister (*RH*, 159). Yet once Floy is established as an unignorable success, Hyacinth pretends that it is her relationship to him that has ensured her triumph: "It is a great thing . . . for a young writer to be *literarily connected*" (*RH*, 177).

Mr. Ellet is not, like Hyacinth, malicious, but instead selfish and unfeeling. Fern's depiction of Ruth's father and her in-laws is part of an exposure of religious hypocrisy that has several manifestations in the novel. While Ruth is properly pious, frequently praying for God's guidance in the days before she is able to rely on herself more than on divine intervention, her relatives use religion for their own ends. When Ruth's father urges her to give her children to Dr. and Mrs. Hall to raise (thus avoiding any responsibility for them on his own part), she quotes a biblical passage about God taking care of fatherless children, thus foiling him "with his own weapons" (*RH*, 68). And when, after sending Katy for what she supposes is a short visit to the Halls, she learns from her father that the couple plans to keep Katy, Ruth muses, "Can *good* people do such things? Is religion only a fable?" (*RH*, 119). The narrow-minded, opinionated Dr. Hall is compared to "the rusty old weather-cock on the village meeting-house, which for twenty years had never been blown about by any whisking wind of doctrine," and domestic disputes with his similarly opinionated wife are avoided only when the two remind each other of "their Calvinistic church obligations to keep the peace" (*RH*, 22). The only reason that Ruth's father and father-in-law agree to provide any financial support to the young widow is that they fear the negative opinions of members of their congregations: "We have a Christian reputation to sustain, brother Ellet," the doctor says piously, and Mr. Ellet is confronted with "a desperate struggle—mammon pulling one way, the church the other" (*RH*, 72). Ruth's natural, intuitive religious belief is thus contrasted with the social conformity of the Ellets and the Halls.

The male characters in *Ruth Hall* who are presented in a positive light act, like Ruth, out of spontaneous human impulse rather than social convention. Emblematic of these is the unnamed "gentleman" who gives Katy money on the street as she returns from visiting her grandfather Ellet. This incident follows closely upon the delivery of flowers to Ruth from Johnny Galt, who had once worked on Ruth and Harry's farm, and both gestures of kindness serve to reinforce the goodness of Harry Hall. The nameless gentleman had been a business associate of Harry who had "learned to love him very much" (*RH*, 89), and Harry had been a generous employer to Johnny Galt. Galt rises to heroic stature later in the novel when, as a fireman, he saves Ruth and her children from a fire. Such coincidence, while characteristic of the popular novel, serves in *Ruth Hall* to emphasize the uncelebrated nature of the selfless act. At the end of the chapter in which the fire occurs, Fanny Fern devotes a paragraph to contrasting public reaction to Johnny's humane action with the reaction to those who send men into battle to be killed. The "butchering, ambitious conqueror" is received with shouts of "bravo! bravo!" while Johnny, after saving Ruth and her daughters from the boardinghouse fire, "crawled to his obscure home, and stretched his weary limbs on his miserable couch." There is also a suggestion that Johnny Galt is intended as a possible suitor for Ruth. Having earlier sent her flowers, he now becomes her rescuing hero. If this pattern is intentional on Fanny Fern's part—and little seems incidental in the novel—then it constitutes one more subversion of the marriage plot, for when Ruth receives the flowers, her remarks center on Johnny's earlier relationship with her small daughter Katy, and there is little evidence to suggest that she even realizes who has rescued her from the fire, because she immediately faints (*RH*, 199).

John Walter is a different kind of heroic figure in the novel. If Ruth Hall is oblivious to the romance plot represented by Johnny Galt, she is instinctively responsive to Walter's offer to advance her career. In keeping with her desire to present Ruth as a woman who seeks support from work rather than from marriage, Fanny Fern develops the relationship between Walter and Ruth as a mutually beneficial professional association. It is significant also that John Walter does not enter Ruth's life until three-fourths of the way through the novel, after Ruth has established her popularity as a columnist. Chapter 67 introduces John Walter, editor of the "Household Messenger," as he muses about the identity of "Floy," whom he regards as a "genius." Walter correctly surmises that Floy writes out of her own personal experiences: furthermore, he perceives the combination of "masculine" and "feminine" qualities that characterize her writing: "what an elastic, strong, brave, loving, fiery, yet soft and winning nature! A bundle of contradictions!" (*RH*, 140). Not only does Walter appreciate Ruth's talents, he is also depicted as a man of high moral principles who believes that good writers have a "moral right to deserved remuneration" (*RH*, 141). When Ruth receives John Walter's letter offering her the chance to write exclusively for his paper, she is initially hesitant; having been taken advantage of by the editors of "The Standard" and "The Pilgrim," she is wary of placing her trust in yet another newspaper editor. But she is quickly won over by Walter's "respectful" tone, by his "bold and manly" handwriting. Ruth's decision to respond to John Walter is influenced by two additional factors that emphasize her independence. One of these is Walter's offer of a "warm, brotherly interest" in her welfare. He replaces the cold, selfish Hyacinth in Ruth's imagination: "how sweet it would be to have him for a brother; a—*real, warm-hearted, brotherly brother*, such as she had never known" (*RH*, 143-44). The other factor is what Ruth has heard about John Walter's own "rags to riches" story, which so closely parallels her own. Instead of a romantic attraction, Ruth and John Walter share an appreciation of each others' struggles.

The female characters whom Fanny Fern views satirically in *Ruth Hall* are, like the male characters, representations of self-interest and hypocrisy. Ruth's mother-in-law, Mrs. Hall, interferes in Ruth's domestic life because she resents losing her son to another woman. "I remember the time when he used to think *me* perfect," Mrs. Hall thinks to herself early in the novel; "I suppose I shall be laid on the shelf now" (*RH*, 18). Her possessive attitude toward her son motivates her efforts to claim "his" children after his death, and this motivation is made clear by the fact that during the time Katy lives with the Halls, her grandmother largely ignores her. In general, women of the upper class, such as Mrs. Hall, are the targets of Fern's satire, whereas servants and working women (with the exception of the nurse, Mrs. Jiff) are portrayed more favorably. Following Harry's death, when Ruth is living in a cheap boardinghouse, two of Ruth's "fashionable friends" (as the chapter title identifies them) discover where she lives, but are too disgusted by her surroundings actually to call on her. The more snobbish of the two remarks that "if Ruth Hall has got down hill so far as this, *I* can't keep up her acquaintance" (*RH*, 81). Miss Skinlin, a dressmaker to the wealthy, is presented as both a gossip and a religious hypocrite, who piously quotes scripture while she steals from her employers. In contrast, Biddy, the Irish nurse whom Ruth had employed to care for her children while Harry was alive, offers to stay on after his death even though Ruth cannot afford to pay her wages. It is no accident that Mrs. Skiddy, certainly not a member of the "fashionable" class, has the most individual strength of any woman in the novel except Ruth herself.

Characters such as Biddy and Mr. and Mrs. Skiddy contribute to one of the strengths of *Ruth Hall* that was largely overlooked by the novel's early critics: its vivid, realistic depiction of midnineteenth-century life. Far from being merely the story of Ruth's fall and rise, Fanny Fern's first novel provides the reader with information about the fashions, dialects, class distinctions, leisure activities, and street scenes that characterized urban life. Despite Fern's claim in her preface that she had "avoided long introductions and descriptions," she is careful to locate the action of her novel in settings that are richly if quickly detailed. The chapter in which Ruth meets Mary Leon at the Beach Cliff Hotel, for example, begins with two paragraphs that establish the bustle of activity at such a seaside resort and underscore the vacant lives of wealthy, "fashionable" people. The hotel guests may amuse themselves with "sails upon the lake," "bathing parties, and horse-back parties"; there are "billiard rooms, and smoking rooms, reading rooms, flirtation rooms." The guests that populate the hotel constitute a panorama of the types for which Fanny Fern had no use—as evidenced in her newspaper columns as well as in *Ruth Hall*: "At Beach Cliff there was the usual number of vapid, fashionable mothers; dressy, brainless daughters; half-fledged wine-bibbing sons; impudent, whisker-dyed roues; bachelors anxious to give their bashfulness an airing; bronchial clergymen in search of health and a text; waning virgins, languishing by candle-light; gouty uncles, dyspeptic aunts, whist-playing old ladies, flirting nursery maids and neglected children" (*RH*, 50). These deft caricatures of the privileged stand in sharp contrast to the sympathetic sketches of the inhabitants of a lower-class neighborhood whom Ruth sees from her boardinghouse window. In the windows of the tenement building across the street, run by "rapacious landlords," Ruth sees a variety of the downtrodden: a tailor and a seamstress doing

piecework at home for low wages, a woman washing clothes, an elderly
woman caring for a sick child. Fern's detail extends to the provisions that
she sees the "ragged procession" purchase from the neighborhood store:
"a few onions, or potatoes, a cabbage, some herrings, a sixpence worth of
poor tea, a pound of musty flour, a few candles, or a peck of coal" (RH,
90). National stereotypes common in the nineteenth century emerge in
this scene as well: the Jewish owner of a neighborhood clothing store is
portrayed as exploiting the hardworking tailor, and a German family in
the tenement building is characterized as "thrifty" (RH, 90).

Fanny Fern's awareness of distinct socioeconomic class divisions in an
increasingly capitalistic American culture permeates Ruth Hall, and
carries with it an implicit set of values that favors the working poor over
the idle upper class. One of the methods that she employs to emphasize
this contrast is to present the views of each group on the same situation.
A case in point is the two chapters regarding Ruth doing her laundry at
the home of her relatives, the Millets, following Harry's death. The
servants in the Millet household feel intense sympathy for Ruth's struggle to support herself and her children and are incensed that the family
for which they work does not provide more assistance to her. Chapter 42
is a conversation between Betty and Gatty, white and black female
servants, in the Millet kitchen. Although, of course, racial and class
distinctions exist between these two women, they are unified in their
belief that their employers—"dese folks of ours, up stairs," as Gatty
says—are behaving selfishly and hypocritically regarding Ruth, noting
that the Millets are sufficiently wealthy to order out-of-season peaches.
Betty recalls how generous Ruth and Harry had been to the Millet
family, bringing them flowers and strawberries from their home in the
country, and the sight of the careworn Ruth saddens and angers both
women. Chapter 44 presents the perspective of the social-climbing
Millets. (The intervening chapter, appropriately enough, is the one
about Johnny Galt and the bouquet of flowers he sends to Ruth—
another reminder of the young couple's generosity.) Mrs. Millet's chatter
to her husband reveals that she makes Ruth provide her own laundry
soap, while the Millets plan to buy their own daughter a $40 velvet
jacket in which to sit for a $300 portrait.

The heartlessness of the headlong rush to climb up the socioeconomic
scale occupied Fanny Fern's attention before she wrote Ruth Hall. An
1853 column in the Olive Branch titled "Dollars and Dimes" is a satiric
response to the notion that "an empty pocket is the worst of crimes."
"Climb, man! climb!" Fern admonishes her readers. "Get to the top of

the ladder, though adverse circumstances and false friends break every round in it! . . . You can use anybody's neck for a footstool, bridle anybody's mouth with a silver bit." Given Fanny Fern's suspicion of the morality of material success, Ruth's own ultimate success might seem ironic or even hypocritical. By the end of the novel, Ruth has made a great deal of money from her first collection of columns and owns 100 shares of bank stock. But success has not altered the moral fiber that Fern established for Ruth early in the novel. In the penultimate chapter, Ruth tells her children that she plans to reward Johnny Galt for his heroism during the fire, and in the last chapter she considers her own mortality as she looks at the "vacant place" beside Harry's grave (*RH*, 211). As if these actions were not enough to assure readers that her heroine has not been corrupted by success, Fanny Fern concludes the novel with the convention of nature's blessing, as "a little bird . . . trilled forth a song as sweet and clear as the lark's at heaven's own blessed gate" (*RH*, 211).

As part of Fanny Fern's satire on pretentiousness, she pays particular attention to women's fashions. The chapter featuring Miss Skinlin, for example, includes a discussion between the seamstress and Mrs. Hall about the proper design of mourning clothes in which decisions about whether the dress should be "gathered or biased" and whether to have a "cross-way fold" on the sleeve assume greater importance than the death of a loved one. Miss Skinlin draws attention to this imbalance when she remarks, "I often feel reproved for aiding and abetting such foolish vanities; and yet, if I refused, from conscientious scruples, to trim dresses, I suppose somebody else *would*" (*RH*, 62). The "fashionable friends" who refuse to call upon Ruth in her boardinghouse turn their conversation to collars as they walk toward a popular luncheon spot, Mary remarking that she had paid $50 for the collar she is wearing, "but what is fifty dollars, when one fancies a thing?" (*RH*, 82). Elsewhere in the novel, Fern also attaches specific dollar amounts to articles of clothing in order to point up the ostentation of the wealthy. At one point, Mrs. Millet comments that her daughter Leila's new silk dress needs more lace and that the $10 this will cost "will not make much difference" in the total cost of the dress. The $10 Mrs. Millet regards as insignificant with regard to Leila's dress is juxtaposed in the same scene to the $10 Harry had paid for a coral pin for Ruth; wanting the pin to wear with her new dress, Leila offers Ruth only $1.25 for it.

Other aspects of Fanny Fern's realism are directed less at her critique of the socioeconomic structure that at this point disadvantages Ruth and more at a revelation of the context of social institutions and belief systems within which her story takes place. The educational system, for example, is the focus of Fern's attention at several points in the novel. The behavior of the young girls at Ruth's boarding school seems to a reader in the late twentieth century remarkably consonant with the theories of Carol Gilligan and other psychologists about the tendency of adolescent girls to abandon notions of individual intellectual achievement in favor of social relationships and acceptability to the opposite sex. Ruth is initially astonished by her peers' habit of sneaking away from their lessons to meet boyfriends; she is, in contrast, the good student, regarded as an "old maid," who writes their compositions for them. But once Ruth becomes convinced of her own physical attractiveness, her attitude becomes the same as theirs, and the language in which Fern describes her transformation suggests that education for young women has little to do with their true vocation: "[S]he had found out her power! . . . *She*, Ruth, could inspire love! Life became dear to her. . . . She had a motive—an aim; she should *some* day make somebody's heart glad,—somebody's hearth-stone bright; somebody should be proud of her; and oh, how she *could* love that somebody! History, astronomy, mathematics, the languages, were all pastime now" (*RH*, 15–16). Although readers now may be tempted to see this passage as ironic, there is little evidence that Fanny Fern intended irony; instead, Ruth's sense of her proper place as a woman, like her identification with flowers and moonbeams early in the novel, is part of her establishment as a conventionally admirable heroine.

Later in *Ruth Hall*, Fern is more openly and directly critical of the educational system, presenting it as plagued by both public inattention and internal dissention. The grim elementary school that Katy attends while she lives with her grandparents is more than just one more evidence of the general bleakness of her life during this period; all of the children suffer from an unventilated, overheated classroom presided over by an unsympathetic teacher, while the attention of the townspeople is focused on other matters, such as the malfunctioning town pump. "What did *they* care that the desks were so constructed, as to crook spines, and turn in toes, and round shoulders? . . . They had other irons in the fire, to which this was a cipher" (*RH*, 138). When Ruth applies to be a primary school teacher, she is submitted to questioning that reveals divisiveness regarding instructional methods. She is questioned about her own education, even to the level of minutiae such as whether she was taught to write on lined or unlined paper, and the scene becomes comic when her examiners, fancifully named "Mr. Fizzle" and "Mr. Squizzle," have a falling out over whether geography is best taught using maps or globes. In the ludicrous conclusion of the examination, the 25 applicants for a single teaching position are required to write an essay on the subject, "was Christopher Columbus standing up, or sitting down, when he discovered America?" (*RH*, 102). Such scenes, although exaggerated to the point of comedy, reveal actual weaknesses in the highly localized school system of the midnineteenth century.

While the sections that deal with education are integrally related to the central plot of the novel, Fanny Fern sometimes presents glimpses of life that seem to arise more from a desire to represent the texture of beliefs and values against which her novel is set. Two such sections concern homeopathic medicine and phrenology—the former a medical treatment that administers doses of substances that would give a healthy person the symptoms of the illness being treated, and the latter a method of ascertaining character and personality by examining the shape of a person's head. Ruth is introduced to homeopathic medicine by a fellow lodger at Mrs. Waters's boardinghouse. Mr. Bond, a quiet, elderly man, offers to treat Ruth's daughter Nettie when she has a fever; though initially reluctant to accept a favor from a stranger, Ruth responds to his "refined and courteous manner" (*RH*, 127), and the treatment is successful. About phrenology, however, Ruth remains skeptical, even though she acquiesces to John Walter's desire to "have [her] head examined" (*RH*, 167). Following the examination by Professor Finman, Ruth comments to Walter that "we have received our $2 worth in flattery" (*RH*, 171), maintaining that "much more is to be told by the expression of people's faces than by the bumps upon their heads" (*RH*, 167). Despite Ruth's dismissal of the phrenological examination as "flattery," the "Professor's" remarks about her serve to establish, from the perspective of an objective, "scientific" source, some of the characteristics that the reader and John Walter have perceived in Ruth: her strong sense of morality, her ability to persevere in the face of adversity, her facility with language, and even her "great powers of sarcasm." It is significant that the phrenologist likens Ruth's writing ability to that of Dickens; Fanny Fern's talent for caricature, and the blending of the melodramatic and the comic in *Ruth Hall*, are similar to those of the British novelist.

Susan Harris has noted that one of Fanny Fern's narrative strategies in *Ruth Hall* is to have Ruth described and assessed by others as a means of underscoring society's power to assess and define women: "Fern's own strategy is to orchestrate a variety of voices, all focused on the central character but all exhibiting their own will to power as they inscribe (and therefore define) the protagonist. The question of voice is at the heart of this novel, then; the work is structured to show, first, how Ruth is defined by the voices of her culture; then, to suggest what kind of voice she might have when she finally begins speaking and writing for herself" (114). By the time of the phrenological examination, which occurs late in the novel, Ruth is fully capable of "speaking for herself," dismissing the phrenologist's "definition" of her. But the phrenologist's assessment is just one of a series of external voices that seek to define Ruth. Her brother, Hyacinth, regards her in childhood as "very plain" and "awkward" (RH, 13), and later as an embarrassing threat to his superiority. Her mother-in-law sees her as frivolous and self-indulgent; her aunt and cousin, as an irritating "poor relation." Ruth is unaware of some of the voices that assess her—voices that contribute to the realism of the novel by representing common attitudes toward women. Two of these voices belong to men who observe Ruth as she moves into one of the boarding-houses she inhabits following Harry's death. Chapter 36 begins with a paragraph of general description of such boarding houses—with their "soiled tablecloths, sticky crockery, oily cookery, bad grammar," "greasy cards," and "bad cigars"—and then shifts from the authorial perspective to that of two male inhabitants who judge Ruth as "prettyish," with a "deuced nice form." Not content with viewing Ruth as an object, one of the men generalizes that "any of the [female] sex may be bought with a yard of ribbon, or a breast pin" (RH, 73–74).

It is against such opinions that Ruth must define her own independence, and one measure of that independence is her freedom and ability to assess others. One of the ways in which Fanny Fern accomplishes this is to have Ruth comment on the writers of letters that "Floy" receives in response to her newspaper columns. In chapter 72, the chapter in which she agrees to the publication of a collection of her columns, shrewdly asking for royalties rather than selling her copyright, Ruth makes no comment on a letter from one Reginald Dabney, who wants Ruth to write a history of his family. But a few chapters later, having stood up to Mr. Tibbets, editor of "The Pilgrim," Ruth expresses her amazement at such requests for her services and critics of her work. A letter from a pompous college professor that ends with the observation that "the *female* mind is incapable of producing anything which may be strictly termed *literature*" does not, as it might have earlier, cause Ruth to doubt her own talent; instead, she dismisses the professor as vain. The only letter that Ruth deems worthy of response is a woman's plea that Ruth take her child should she die in childbirth. The third group of letters, in chapter

80, all praise Ruth's work and arrive in the same mail with the news that her book is a great success. These external voices all confirm the power of Ruth's own voice in her columns; even the condescending professor has been moved to write by Ruth's wide popularity with her readers.

The critical reception that *Ruth Hall* would receive upon its publication in December 1854 is foreshadowed several times in the novel. In conversation with John Walter following her phrenological examination, Ruth reveals that she does not object to "fair criticism" of her work, but she is outraged by reviewers who do not bother to read the books they write about or who quote passages out of context. It is clear in Ruth's speech at this point that unfair reviews raise questions of gender as well as of ethics; a woman whose work is thus reviewed, she says, "must either weep in silence over such injustice, or do violence to her womanly nature by a public contention for her rights" (*RH*, 172). An even more specific foreshadowing of response to the novel occurs in Ruth's confrontation with Mr. Tibbets about her decision to write exclusively for a rival newspaper. Angered by what he perceives as her ingratitude, Tibbets twice threatens her in terms that suggest William Moulton's *The Life and Beauties of Fanny Fern*. Tibbets first says that he will usurp her plans for a collection of her columns by publishing a "cheap edition" of her work himself, and when she points out that her own publisher would not allow such an infringement of its contractual rights, Tibbets resorts to a critical threat: "When you see a paragraph in print that will sting your proud soul to the quick, know that John Tibbets has more ways than one of humbling so imperious a dame" (*RH*, 157). *The Life and Beauties of Fanny Fern* is much longer than a "paragraph," but it does include a number of Fanny Fern's columns. The ability to predict reactions to her own work so closely demonstrates the author's understanding of the position of the woman writer in the midnineteenth century.

The reviews of *Ruth Hall* were by no means uniformly negative. Although the novel was attacked by some on the grounds of its author's "unwomanly" satiric portraits of members of her own family, other reviewers found much to praise. It was called "a thrilling life sketch," "a fresh racy volume," and "a book of extraordinary interest." Some reviewers emphasized the novel's potential for moral uplift. "Read it, you cannot fail to be the better of it," urged the *Pittsburg Family Journal*, and the *Schoharie Democrat* characterized the novel as "a real *Heart Book*, a household book." The reviewer for the *New York Tribune* perhaps came closest to the assessment of more recent critics by noting that "flashes of gayest humor alternate with bursts of deep pathos." Recent analyses of nineteenth-century women's fiction and reassessments of the history of American realism have provided means of understanding *Ruth Hall* that were unavailable to its contemporary critics. By focusing on the claiming of one's own language as a precondition of autonomy, by resisting the closure of the "marriage plot" and by establishing her heroine within the matrix of authentic nineteenth-century culture, Fanny Fern made a major contribution to the tradition of American fiction.

Chapter Four
Rose Clark

Most scholars and commentators who bother to mention at all Fanny Fern's second novel, *Rose Clark*, assume that this novel owes its more conventional characteristics to the author's desire to avoid the storm of controversy surrounding the publication of *Ruth Hall* in 1854. Whether or not this was the case, it is true that *Rose Clark*, published in December 1856, more nearly conforms to the standards of the midnineteenth-century domestic novel. Its title character is a far more conventional heroine than is Ruth Hall; the plot relies heavily on coincidence; and the style and scenes are frequently melodramatic. Yet despite the fact that *Rose Clark* lacks many of the qualities that distinguish *Ruth Hall*, it nevertheless embodies elements of Fanny Fern's social criticism, and contains autobiographical material not included in her first novel. Furthermore, although Rose Clark is the pure and passive heroine common in the women's novels of the period, her friend Gertrude Dean is much like Ruth Hall in her strength and independence of mind.

An "Unpretending Story"

The author's preface to *Ruth Hall* is significant for the manner in which it foretells Fern's use of the methodology of realism; the preface to *Rose Clark* is striking because the author is explicit about the fact that this work should not be considered "literature." Instead, she terms it an "unpretending story," and describes the family setting in which it is to be read: "When the frost curtains the windows, when the wind whistles fiercely at the key-hole, when the bright fire glows, and the tea-tray is removed, and father in his slippered feet lolls in his arm-chair; and mother with her nimble needle 'makes auld claes look amaist as weel as new,' and grandmamma draws closer to the chimney-corner, and Tommy with his plate of chestnuts nestles contentedly at her feet; . . . For such an hour, for such an audience, was it written."

This cozy, albeit stereotypically domestic, scene has a warmth and vitality that is in sharp contrast to "literature" and its readers: "Should any *dictionary on legs* rap importunely at the door for admittance, send him away to the groaning shelves of some musty library, where 'literature' lies embalmed, with its stony eyes, fleshless joints, and ossified heart, in flawless preservation." Nina Baym suggests that the language of Fern's preface, by making "immortal" literature a corpse, "justifies the kind of immediate, functional writing she herself does" (33). Baym's comments are part of her point that women writers at midcentury consistently denied that what they created should be judged by the standards of "art," thus making it difficult for women of later generations to be taken seriously as artists. Yet given Fanny Fern's often-stated rejection of anything pompous or pretentious, it seems likely that her preface to *Rose Clark* is also one more statement favoring a genuinely interested reader over a staid scholar or critic.

Indeed, it is easy to imagine such a family group as Fern pictures being caught up in the story of Rose Clark. Little Tommy, for example, would feel fortunate not to live in the orphanage to which Rose, at age six, is sent following the death of her mother. In this "charity-school," presided over by the matron, Mrs. Markham, children are denied virtually everything children need: fresh air, exercise, and good food. Nor do Rose's fortunes improve appreciably when she is taken to live with her Aunt Dolly a few years later. Ruth's mother's sister, who runs a millinery shop, views Rose as as source of cheap labor, and denies her the education for which she yearns. Throughout this miserable childhood, Rose remains a "good" girl, never openly defying either Mrs. Markham or her aunt. Thus it comes as a surprise, in chapter 19, to find 16-year-old Rose traveling in a coach with her infant son; not only does she seem not to have a husband, but a subsequent chapter leads the reader to believe that Rose had been the victim of a "seduced and abandoned" plot, as a brash young man named Vincent boasts of his conquest of a young girl. Apparently, Rose's Aunt Dolly also believes her to be a fallen woman, because Dolly sends her a letter of dismissal that begins, "You must be aware that you have built up a wall between yourself and the virtuous of your own sex; you must know that you have no claim upon the love or sympathy of any such."[1]

The rest of the novel deals with Rose's struggle to find her missing husband and reinstate her virtue. Only in the last chapters of the novel do we learn that Rose's marriage to Vincent (a cousin to the young cynic of the same name introduced in an earlier chapter) is indeed legal, that Vincent has been confined first to a poorhouse and then to a lunatic asylum as the result of an accident on the road that caused him to lose his memory, and that he has spent the ensuing years looking for Rose. Rose, meanwhile, has selected New Orleans as the site of her search, for no apparent reason except a "magnetism which had drawn her thither" (*RC*, 203). There she meets briefly a woman that the evil cousin Vincent has ruined, and, still believing there to be only one Vincent L'Estrange Vincent, later reads in a newspaper that he has been poisoned in "a house of questionable reputation" in Natchez (*RC*, 213).

Thus, midway through the novel, Rose believes herself to be a widow, but she resists the proposals of kind Dr. Perry, who has fallen in love with her on the way to New Orleans, because of her loyalty to Vincent. Coincidences abound in this latter half of the novel. Dr. Perry (whose first name is Walter on page 277, but is otherwise John) turns out to be the long-lost brother of Gertrude Dean, an artist who lives in Rose's apartment building; Chloe, the black nurse assigned to take care of Rose when she becomes ill after reading about what she supposes is her husband's murder, is the freed former slave of the evil Vincent's wealthy mother; when Rose, Gertrude, and John Perry take a trip to Niagara Falls, Gertrude's ex-husband, whom she has not seen for years, happens to be there as well, and John happens to overhear a conversation that identifies him. Meanwhile, Rose's husband Vincent stumbles upon the home of a Mrs. Bond, who considered Rose her own child after Charley was born, and thus learns that Rose was still true to him; next, he boards the same ship that had taken Rose to New Orleans, and thus picks up her trail again; finally, six years after Charley's birth, a remark overheard in a cafe restores Vincent to Rose.

The couple are happily reunited, and with their son, Charley, the family circle is complete. The novel thus follows the marriage plot that Fanny Fern had rejected in *Ruth Hall*; *Rose Clark*'s patience and piety are rewarded with the restoration of her husband, and the novel ends on a note of rosy optimism for the future, with the "scales of eternal justice" balanced by the power of God. Late in the novel, Gertrude Dean observes of Vincent's story that it is "so singular . . . that in a novel it would be stigmatized as incredible, overdrawn, and absurd" (*RC*, 405), and this statement could be used to characterize the plot of the novel as a whole.

Good and Bad Women

Whereas *Ruth Hall*'s strengths are her perseverance and her talent, *Rose Clark*'s strengths are her conventional goodness and piety. In *Ruth Hall*, Fern identifies her central character with flowers and moonbeams just long enough so that these codes of the sentimental novel would create sympathy for Ruth in the contemporary reader. Rose Clark, by contrast, is identified with such images of pure womanhood throughout the novel—most overtly in her name. Rose's womanly modesty is established in the first chapter when, upon her admission to the orphanage at age six, she refuses to allow the matron's assistant to see her naked. Throughout the novel, Rose blushes easily and frequently, and is provided with the pale skin that makes this more obvious. She wins the heart of Mrs. Clifton, the wife of the minister, when she puts flowers on the grave of the Cliftons' dead infant, and Rose's own son, Charley, is also associated with flowers, such as the ones that Gertrude scatters around him as she begins to sketch him, calling him "sweet and holy enough for an Infant Savior" (*RC*, 220).

Interestingly, some of the "evil" characters in *Rose Clark* are shown to have an aversion to flowers, especially the two women who make Rose's early life miserable. Mrs. Markham, who makes life as grim as possible for the children at the orphanage, objects to her assistant, Timmins, putting a bouquet of flowers on Mrs. Markham's desk on the day the committee of overseers are due to visit, calling it "green trash" and "a frivolous thing." When Timmins points out that God has seen fit to put flowers all over this world, Mrs. Markham's only reply is "Pshaw!" (*RC*, 48–49). Rose's Aunt Dolly, a milliner by profession, shares this dislike of flowers. When the minister, Mr. Clifton, attempts to bring cheer to the life of young Rose, who is little more than a servant in her aunt's house, he asks Dolly whether Rose likes flowers. Her reply attempts to dissociate Rose as well as herself from this emblem of female purity—a foreshadowing of her later designation of Rose as a fallen woman: "I guess not . . . I am sure I never could see any use in them, except to make artificial ones by, to trim bonnets." (*RC*, 79).

Both Mrs. Markham and Aunt Dolly value the utilitarian over the artistic, duty over creativity, and the central manifestation of each woman's preference is a dislike of books. For both of these women, books represent a frivolity and dreamy romanticism they believe to be at odds with their commonsense lives. Describing Mrs. Markham's richly appointed parlor—a room that contrasts sharply with the Spartan living quarters of the orphans—Fanny Fern notes that there were ". . . for the look of the thing, a few books, newspapers, pamphlets, etc., for Mrs. Markham never read; partly because she had a surfeit in the book line in the school-room, but principally, because publishers and editors had a sad way of making their types so indistinct now-a-days; or in other words, Markham had a strong aversion to spectacles" (*RC*, 39–40). In Markham's case, vanity is the source of her aversion to books; in the case of Dolly, it is jealousy. Dolly associates books with her deceased sister Maria, Rose's mother, whom she has resented most of her life. The differences between the two sisters—Maria intellectual, Dolly (as her name suggests) vain—emerged early in their lives; according to Dolly, "[Maria] was after every book she could find, before she could speak plain, and when she got hold of one, you might fire off a pistol in the room, and she wouldn't hear it. . . . Why, you never saw any thing like our Maria. She went and sold the only silk gown she had to buy a grammar and dictionary, to learn what she acknowledged was a dead language" (*RC*, 35). Dolly is particularly bothered by those aspects of Rose that remind her of Maria, and her most severe and consistent criticism of Rose is that she is just like her mother. In addition to a shared love of books, Maria and Rose are alike in quickly winning the affection of other people, a fact that the lonely Dolly especially resents: "I declare . . . our Maria was the beater for one thing; every body who ever saw her used to carry on about her just like that child; even the cats and dogs liked a kick from her better than a petting from any body else, and as to her husband, he thought the mold was broke (as that image man said) after his wife was made" (*RC*, 87–88). Fanny Fern makes it clear in Dolly's remark that the one part of Maria's life she is most jealous of is her happy marriage to Professor Clark. For despite their apparent single-mindedness about their professions, both Aunt Dolly and Mrs. Markham (who is presumably a widow) yearn to be married. Despite Dolly's disdainful remark about Maria that "she couldn't have earned her living to have saved her life, if she hadn't got married" (*RC*, 68)—a remark that reminds the reader that marriage was an economic necessity for most nineteenth-century women—Dolly tells her friend Kip that "it is dull work for a woman to live all her life alone" (*RC*, 37). And, like the stereotypical husband-hunting spinster of so much nineteenth-century humor, she vows to find a husband:

> "I will own it to *you*, Kip, I mean to get married!"
> "You don't!" screamed Kip; "to whom?"
> "Lord knows, I don't, but I feel sure I shall do it."
> "How?" asked Kip, with great interest.
> "Never you mind," said Dolly. (*RC*, 38).

Fanny Fern plays out the stereotype by having Dolly show momentary interest in a man whose wife has just died, only to change her mind when she discovers that the widower has 10 children (*RC*, 89); later in the novel a seamstress named Miss Bodkin rehearses Dolly's history for a friend, emphasizing her pursuit of men: "Such a fidget as it was in to get its name changed; but nobody seemed to want it. It tried the minister, it tried the deacon, it tried the poor, bony old sexton (mercy knows it never would have taken such pains, had it known as much about men as I do), however, that's neither here nor there. . . . Well—by and by a shoe-maker from the city came up to our village for three weeks' fishing, and while he was baiting for fish, Dolly baited for him" (*RC*, 177). The shoemaker, later turned successful businessman, is John Howe.

Throughout *Rose Clark*, the novelist provides glimpses of the marriage of Dolly and John Howe. As was the case with several such relationships in *Ruth Hall*, Fern's purpose is to show that not all marriages are the "happily ever after" variety, and to provide some of her usual satire on various cultural "types." The Howes' marriage is essentially a struggle for power between a vain and manipulative woman and a good-hearted man who is initially cowed by his wife but eventually gains the upper hand. The materialistic tendencies that caused Dolly to cheat her own customers when she worked as a milliner are given free rein when she marries the wealthy Howe; she slavishly follows fashions, orders her servants around, and has fantasies of a family coat-of-arms. Her favorite visitor is a foppish poet named Finels, who flatters her outrageously and laughs at her behind her back. The essential goodness of John Howe is first evident when he attempts to defy his wife's orders and move Rose and her son from a grim attic to a comfortable guest room when Charley is ill. Later in the novel he is identified with "an unpolished, but good-hearted country cousin" named Jonathan, a conventional represen-tation of rural purity and simplicity that is in contrast with the artifici-ality associated with Dolly's social-climbing friends. The turning point in the Howes' relationship occurs when they are in a train wreck while on a trip to Saratoga; Dolly is humiliated by the loss of her false teeth, and John takes the opportunity to vent the rage that he has felt for so long: "From that journey Mr. Howe dated his final and triumphant Declara-tion of Domestic Independence. The spell of Mrs. Howe's cabalistic whisper was broken. Mr. Howe had a counter-spell. Mrs. Howe's day was over" (*RC*, 263).

Both Dolly Howe and Mrs. Markham (who is not successful in her search for a husband) come to bad and rather melodramatic ends in the novel—punishment for their torture of Fanny Fern's heroine Rose. Dolly is the victim of her own willful innocence about the attentions of the parasitic Finels. As John Howe begins to devote more of his money to gambling and less to his wife, she is less able to provide Finels with the luxuries that had always constituted his interest in her; when Finels turns his attentions elsewhere, Dolly turns to drink, and she ultimately dies of delirium tremens, "shrieking for 'John,' and 'Rose,' and 'Finels,' and the deuce knows who" (*RC*, 367). Mrs. Markham's abuse of her orphaned charges is finally discovered by the head of the committee of overseers when he makes a surprise visit. She is fired from her job and disappears from the novel until the final chapter, when, reduced to a "bundle of rags," she is discovered in the street outside Rose's house, and dies in Rose's arms, her final words a plea for forgiveness: "Oh! God forgive me! Mercy! mercy!" Rose, whose face is described as "pitying as God's angels," asks that God grant her wish, "even at the eleventh hour" (*RC*, 416).

Another melodramatic element of *Rose Clark* is the frequent deaths of infants and small children—an echo of Sara Willis's loss of her daughter in 1845. Shortly after Rose enters Mrs. Markham's orphanage, one of the other little girls dies, apparently a victim of Markham's neglect. The infant child of the Reverend Clifton and his wife dies shortly after Rose comes to live with Dolly, and Dolly's own infant daughter dies on the day she is to be christened. None of these deaths, however, is purely gratuitous; each serves to make a moral point. The death in the orphanage points up Mrs. Markham's neglect of the youngsters placed in her care and her scorn for the children of the poor. The death in the parsonage helps to reinforce Rose's caring nature, as she strews flowers on the infant's grave. And Dolly Howe's loss of her daughter is the first step in Fanny Fern's punishment of her for her treatment of Rose, as the close of the chapter makes clear: "'Vengeance is mine—I will repay, saith the Lord'" (*RC*, 188).

Social Commentary

Despite the overtly melodramatic elements and the plot's heavy reliance on coincidence, *Rose Clark*, like *Ruth Hall*, contains numerous passages of social commentary that reflect the values Fanny Fern expressed in her newspaper columns. In both her character portrayals and direct addresses to the reader, she provides sharp commentary on greed, hypocrisy, the shallowness of conventional religion, disparities between social classes, and other matters of concern to an observer of the increasingly mercantile culture of the midnineteenth century. Melodrama and social critique were a common mixture in fiction of the 1840s and 1850s, and Stephen Knadler has suggested that the purpose of such melodramatic or sentimental novels may sometimes have been different from the moral point about purity and the justice of God that is clearly central to Fanny Fern's intent here. In his study of Melville's novel *Pierre*, Knadler proposes that sensational fiction of the period, with its melodramatic plot elements akin to the murder of the "bad" Vincent and the deaths of Mrs. Markham and Dolly Howe, appealed to the laboring class because they "gave imaginative expression to the anxiety and frustrations of the new underclass, . . . and, more importantly, provided the coordinates around which these working men and women would become aware of themselves as a common disenfranchised group."[2] By showing that even the affluent could lose their lands or their inheritances and end up in the Bowery, such fiction countered the liberal ideology that posited stable success as the inevitable reward for hard work.

Although Rose survives the rigors of her childhood and is last seen as a contented wife and mother, her survival is due to chance rather than industry, as is the case with Ruth Hall. Not only the grim repression of the orphanage, but—more important—the philosophy of poverty that underlies it demonstrate some of the misconceptions that ensured the perpetuation of a lower class. From the first pages of the novel, it is clear that those in power, such as Mrs. Markham and her committee, regard the poor as a breed apart, responsible for their own misfortune. When told Rose's name, Mrs. Markham remarks, "I knew it would be sure to be something fanciful; beggars always go on stilts" (*RC*, 15), and after cutting off Rose's lovely hair, she says with satisfaction that Rose looks "more befitting [her] condition" (*RC*, 16). When the lack of good food, fresh air, and exercise takes its toll on the health of the children, the overseers blame heredity: "At stated times, the committee came in to look at them, and remarked how inevitably children of the lower classes inherited poor constitutions from their depraved parents, and went away as satisfied as if, granting this to be the case, they were humanly endeavoring to remedy the inherited curse; as if they were not keeping those growing limbs in overstrained positions for hours, and depriving them of the blessed air and sunshine, which God intended childhood to revel in as freely as the birds and flowers" (*RC*, 32–33).

The sarcasm of this passage gives way to a vehement address to the reader a few chapters later, when Fanny Fern generalizes from this orphan-school to education in general, exhorting parents to make visits to their children's schools, "not on farce exhibition days, but by unexpected calls, at such times as he or she may see fit" (*RC*, 50), in order to see whether such abuse exists. Always an advocate of children, Fern wrote in her newspaper columns about the need to avoid lesser abuses of children than the physical and emotional debilitation of the orphanage. One of the essays in her 1868 collection *Folly As It Flies* is titled "Children have their Rights"; the essay begins with the observation, "There is not a day of my life in which I am not vexed at the injustice done to children" (*FF*, 232). The injustices to which Fern refers in the essay are not life-threatening; taken together, they amount to not treating children with respect as *people*: forcing them to kiss strangers or eat foods they abhor; failing to respect their privacy or expecting them to use good manners when they are not treated correspondingly.

As she does in *Ruth Hall*, Fanny Fern devotes considerable attention to disparities between social classes, master and servants, the upwardly mobile and the poor in *Rose Clark*. Here, as in her first novel, those lower on the socioeconomic ladder are generally more virtuous than are those near the top, as though both the desire to improve one's material condition and wealth itself are corrupting influences. One remarkable contrast is that drawn between Rose's Aunt Dolly and Mrs. Bond, with whom Rose lives for a short while after Charley is born and Dolly rejects her. Even when she runs her small millinery shop in Difftown, Dolly's greed makes her cheat her customers by making them pay for more material than is needed for their hats. Marriage to John Howe and a move to the city only intensify Dolly's desire to be socially powerful, but her own seamstress, Miss Bodkin, sees through her pretensions to the real person. Setting out to tell her friend Miss Snecker about Dolly's history—"what caterpillar that butterfly came from," as she puts it—Miss Bodkin notes that "Mrs. John Howe" is "a very well sounding name, you see, but for all that it never can make a lady of her" (*RC*, 176–77).

For Dolly Howe, being a "lady" is all a matter of appearances: having a carriage, shopping at the best stores, wearing expensive clothes, and vacationing at the "right" places. Unimaginative and gullible, Dolly is a slave to flattery—from the dress shop owner who tells her that she looks good in lilac and from the foppish Finels, who pretends to find her sensitive to poetry. Just as she prefers artificial flowers to natural ones, she lives by artifice rather than by feeling. When she is attempting to convince her husband to take a trip to Saratoga Springs—the trip on which John Howe finally refuses to be bullied anymore—she remarks that "it is so vulgar to stay in the city in summer," and in response to

John's comment that some "fashionables" merely shut up their houses and pretend to be gone, she says, "even that is better than to be thought unfashionable" (*RC*, 210). Dolly's obsession with what others will think of her proves to be her undoing, for when Finels finds someone younger and wealthier to flatter, her only recourse is alcohol.

Mrs. Bond, by contrast, is an unpretentious country woman who is as closely identified with the natural as Dolly is with the artificial: "She never treads on the little ant-houses in the gravel walks, she says the robins have earned a right to the cherries by keeping the insects from the trees, she has turned veterinary surgeon to keep the breath of life in an old skeleton of a horse, . . . she puts crumbs on the piazza for the ground birds, and is very careful to provide for the motherly yellow cat a soft bed" (*RC*, 174). Though far from wealthy, Mrs. Bond is charitable. She responds with quick sympathy to Rose's plight, and the two develop a mother–daughter relationship. Fittingly, it is to Mrs. Bond's house that Vincent comes accidentally when he is searching for Rose, although he does not tell her who he is. Fanny Fern makes explicit the contrast between Dolly Howe's artifice and Mrs. Bond's natural goodness when the latter makes a rare visit to the unspecified "city" where Dolly lives: "Its kaleidoscope frivolities had little charm for Mrs. Bond; her necessary wants were supplied from the village, and she was so fortunate as to have no artificial ones" (*RC*, 129). Just as their lives are in contrast, so too the deaths of the two women differ markedly. Whereas Dolly is last seen in the throes of delirium tremens, being hauled off to jail by a policeman, Mrs. Bond dies peacefully, and Fern describes the "pleasant afternoon sunshine" on her "placid" face (*RC*, 395).

Most of the other characters who are neither part of nor yearn to be part of the "fashionable" class are portrayed as having more human kindness than those who are caught up in the pre–Civil War frenzy for the trappings of gentility. Both Mrs. Markham and Dolly Howe have assistants in their professional lives who try, in their limited ways, to make their employers more humane. Timmins, who works in the or-phanage, cares for the children as Markham does not and is rewarded by being called a "fool." Superstitious and ill-educated, Timmins nonethe-less knows that the children are being emotionally and physically de-prived and apparently has known such deprivation herself. When trying to comfort the newly arrived Rose, she remarks, "you are not the only person who has had a hard time of it. I was a little girl once" (*RC*, 23). When Rose comments that she does not hear any noise of play from the other children, Timmins thinks to herself, "I wish to the land Mrs.

Markham had heard you say that" (*RC*, 25), but she fears Markham's wrath, so that her rebellion is no more open than putting a vase of flowers on Markham's desk. Similarly, Dolly's millinery assistant Daffy (for "Daffodil") dares only mildly reproach her employer. When, for example, Dolly schemes to have her customers pay for more material and ribbon than is necessary so that Dolly can use the extra for herself, Daffy merely says, "Sometimes I think it isn't right" (*RC*, 93). But shortly thereafter, in a soliloquy, Daffy bursts out, "It's awful to hold in when a body's so rampageous mad. . . . Dolly has no more heart than that pine table." But expressing her anger to Dolly would be risky: "I wish I dared tell her so to her face—but it isn't in me; she makes me shrivel all up, when she puts on one of her horrid looks, and I can't be looking for a new place with this rheumatism fastening on me every time the wind blows" (*RC*, 100). The timidity with which these members of the laboring class must approach the immorality of their employers is yet another reminder of the precarious economic condition of single women in the nineteenth century.

The one instance of a servant who is herself conniving and hypocritical emerges also from this economic reality. Miss Anne Cooper, "a maiden lady of forty-two," is the servant of Madame Vincent, mother of the "bad" Vincent and aunt of Rose's husband. She expects to be one of the wealthy Madame Vincent's heirs, but the longer the elderly woman lives, the more entitled Anne feels to steal from her mistress, who seems determined to live many more years. To ensure her eventual inheritance, Anne is careful to flatter Madame Vincent in an "oily, hypocritical whine which is inseparable from your genuine toady, be it man or woman" (*RC*, 295). Anne is even more resentful of her status as a servant because of the fact that she had been secretly in love with young Vincent, now deceased, but cannot openly mourn him. When Madame Vincent becomes determined to adopt Rose's son, Charley, because he so closely resembles her dead son, Anne realizes that the boy would become Madame Vincent's heir, and she tells her employer that Rose is scheming to get money from her in exchange for Charley, in order to dissuade her from her plan.

In addition to addressing the uneasy relations among social classes in an increasingly capitalistic society, Fanny Fern also comments in this novel, as she had in *Ruth Hall*, on the differences between effective and ineffective ministers, true religious commitment and sham hypocritical piety. Because *Rose Clark* is a far more conventional novel than *Ruth Hall*, much of the responsibility for reward and punishment alike is assigned to God—indeed, the last line of the novel, following the death of Mrs.

Markham, is "God is just!" (RC, 417). In keeping with her characterization as a "true woman," Rose is unfailingly convinced of the goodness of
God, despite her many trials, and the Reverend Clifton, who attempts to
befriend Rose in Difftown, is the quintessential "good" minister—
hardworking, caring, and sincere: "He loved his calling—it was not
mere lip service for him to expound the word of God, and teach its sacred
truths—the humblest among his people knew this; the tremor in his
voice, the moisture in his eye, told their own eloquent tale" (RC, 72). Yet
even in her initial description of Reverend Clifton, Fanny Fern is careful
to distinguish him from the kind of minister who is more concerned with
himself than with the welfare of his flock. In fact, she writes that he was
"one of those few clergymen who possessed of decided talent was yet
content to labor in an humble sphere." Others had "left their country
parishes to become stars in cities," where, "inflated with pride and
self-conceit, [they] preached soft things to those who build them palaces
of ease" (RC, 71). Lest this be seen merely as a rural-urban dichotomy,
later in the novel Gertrude Dean expounds on the difference between the
ministers of Boston and those of New York. In the latter city, she says,
"churches are . . . shut up in the summer months, while the minister
luxuriates in the country at his ease" (RC, 371).

   If Clifton and Rose are the novel's most outstanding examples of true
religious devotion, the best exemplar of hypocritical piety is John Stahle,
Gertrude's second husband, who, like Ruth's parents and in-laws in *Ruth
Hall*, maintains a worshipful facade to conceal his mean-spiritedness.
Even while abusing her and her child, Gertrude says, "he had a religious
character to sustain": "during all this time he was more constant than
ever, if that were possible, at every church and vestry-meeting, often
taking part in the exercises, and always out-singing and out-praying
every other church member" (RC, 252). Stahle's false piety is part of his
plot to force her to leave him while he appears to be the offended party,
but the plot backfires. Stahle is overheard plotting against Gertrude in
Niagara Falls, and her brother confronts him and sends him away; when
Gertrude expresses her fear that he will retaliate, John answers that "his
Christian reputation stands in the way of any such little personal grati-
fication" (RC, 350).

   Interestingly, in a novel that features such a stereotypical sentimental
heroine as Rose, Fanny Fern devotes much more time to commentary on
social injustices to women than she had in *Ruth Hall*. Even though two of
the central villains of *Rose Clark* are women—Mrs. Markham and Dolly
Howe—the author takes pains to point out several ways in which social

attitudes and the legal system discriminate against women—and, further, to suggest that certain social attitudes toward women both underlie and perpetuate an unfair system of laws. The twin stereotypes of women as inherently virtuous and as the seducers of men, for example, led Victorian culture to at once venerate and fear them; innocence was presumed to make women incapable of owning or managing property, while the resulting economic dependence created the image of woman as overtly materialistic. Such are the attitudes that emerge in the conversation between the "bad" Vincent and his friend Grey in chapter 20 of *Rose Clark*. Vincent, in boasting of his conquest of a "boarding-school girl" (whom the reader at this point supposes to be Rose), makes a distinction between innocence and virtue, using "innocence" in the sense of "ignorance." The girl was "primevally innocent" enough to believe that Vincent had married her, but Vincent does not believe that virtuous women exist; he says to Grey, "no woman, my dear boy, was ever virtuous but for lack of temptation and opportunity" (*RC*, 120). When Grey, who is shocked at this statement, leaves the room, Vincent calls him "green," and muses on the logic of his own beliefs: "If women are virtuous, why do they give the cold shoulder to steady moral fellows, to smile on a reckless dog like me? I have always found women much more anxious to ascertain the state of a man's purse than the state of his morals" (*RC*, 121). Women who are assumed to have lost their "virtue" are shown in the novel to be scorned by men and women alike. The predecessor of the young schoolgirl about whom Vincent boasts to his friend is the same young woman whom Rose encounters soon after her arrival in New Orleans (and presumably the one who kills him in Natchez). Described in Fern's chapter subtitle as a "maniac," she seems in the text merely a woman distraught and frustrated by Vincent's deceit and society's dismissal of her: "The 'good' closed their doors, and said 'Stand aside, I am holier than thou'; the bad opened theirs, and said, 'Eat, drink, and be merry'" (*RC*, 205). Of having poisoned Vincent, she merely says, "Men make the laws to suit themselves, so they make no law for the seducer" (*RC*, 206). Rose can sympathize with being shunned as a "fallen" woman: not only has her Aunt Dolly rejected her, but the servant at Mrs. Bond's house refuses to help her with her laundry, and her landlady in New Orleans tries to evict her until Gertrude intercedes.

Gertrude Dean's story of mistreatment is perhaps the most terrible—and certainly the longest—in the novel. The story Gertrude tells of her past introduces an autobiographical element missing from *Ruth Hall*: Sara Willis's disastrous marriage to Samuel Farrington. As Mary Kelley notes, "As if she could not avoid it, Parton/Fern appeared to be forever caught in double, if delayed, exposure" (266). Despite her efforts to conceal even the fact of her second marriage, much less its details, Parton/Fern may have felt it necessary to put in print her side of the story, because one of the most painful aspects of her relationship with Farrington was the rumors he spread about her. Whatever the reason for including this account, by doing so Fanny Fern introduces the most interesting character in the novel, the one who is most like Ruth Hall, and the one who serves as the spokesperson for Fanny Fern's views. Gertrude makes her living as a painter rather than as a writer, but her personal history, her independent spirit, and her confidence in speaking her mind mark her as a kindred spirit to Ruth Hall/Fanny Fern.

Unlike Ruth Hall (although like Rose Clark), Gertrude was orphaned when young and was raised by a distant relative in a variant of the Cinderella story with "stepsisters" who trade her beloved books for ribbon. Like Ruth Hall, she has an older brother, whom she has not seen for years (Dr. John Perry, with whom she is reunited in the novel), and, like Ruth, her first marriage is an extremely happy one: "Never was a wife blessed with a truer heart to rest upon—never was a wife nearer forgetting that happiness is but the exception in this world of change" (RC, 230). After five years and the birth of a son, her husband dies, and she struggles to support herself. Rather than detailing that period, Gertrude says to Rose, "Why weary you with a repetition of its repulses—of my humiliations, and struggles, and vigils?" (RC, 231)— and to the reader of Ruth Hall it would be repetition indeed.

Few details of Sara Willis's marriage to Samuel Farrington have survived, so it is impossible to know whether or how much Fanny Fern embellished this part of her life in Gertrude's story. However, like Farrington, John Stahle is a widower with two children, and like Sara Willis, Gertrude is initially opposed to the idea of marrying him: "My heart recoiled at the thought, for my husband was ever before me" (RC, 231). Finally persuaded that Stahle will provide her child with a good home, she reluctantly accepts his proposal, with the stipulation that the marriage not be consummated. Sensing Gertrude's lukewarm commitment to the relationship, Stahle secretly places an announcement of their marriage in a newspaper, and thus tricks her into an immediate wedding ceremony—Gertrude filled with foreboding and dressed, appropriately, in black. Gertrude soon becomes aware that Stahle is "a hypocrite, and a gross sensualist. That it was passion, not love, which he felt for me, and

that marriage was only the stepping stone to an else impossible gratifi-
cation" (*RC*, 235).

What this melodramatic language indicates is that the first offense
that Stahle enacts against Gertrude is what would today be called wife
abuse or marital rape. The source of Gertrude's (and Fanny Fern's) anger
about this and Stahle's later offenses is that all of them are legal—that
women are not protected from various kinds of abuse by their husbands.
Gertrude's only recourse is to make sure that she is herself blameless in
the relationship so that he cannot accuse her of any failure to perform her
wifely duties: "The more my heart recoiled, the more strict was my
outward observance" (*RC*, 236). But her compliance merely angers
Stahle; he needs an adversary, and she refuses to be one. After Gertrude
has won the love of his children, Stahle abruptly sends them away; when
she proves to be a good, frugal homemaker, he insists that they give up
their house and live in boardinghouses, where he makes certain that the
servants ignore her and tries to trick her into appearing to be unfaithful
to him. When both Gertrude and her son need medical attention, Stahle
refuses to assist them. Yet as severe as these abuses are, the one which
seems to Gertrude the most serious infringement of her rights is Stahle's
reading of her personal letters; this is the only time she challenges him,
to which he responds, "the law says you can have nothing that is not
mine." Gertrude/Fanny Fern follows Stahle's response with the statement, "O, how many crushed and bleeding hearts all over our land can
endorse the truth of this brutal answer" (*RC*, 251).

Unable to trick Gertrude into any action that would be grounds for
divorce, Stahle devises an elaborate plan to charge her with desertion.
He, in fact, leaves her, but subsequently sends her letters requesting that
she join him in another city—without her son—and meanwhile spreads
rumors to make it look as if he was justified in leaving. Even though
Stahle's plan succeeds, and he obtains a divorce from Gertrude on the
grounds of desertion, he remains obsessed with her, watching for any
sign of weakness. But instead of giving in to despair, or marrying the first
man who asks her, Gertrude discovers her talent as an artist, and soon
achieves a reputation as a fine painter, her fortunes rising as those of
Stahle decline. When John Perry overhears his conversation with a friend
on the porch of a Niagara hotel, Stahle is expressing his dismay at this
outcome: "I thought when I left her that she would just fold her hands,
and let the first man who offered find her in clothes, on his own terms, for
she never was brought up to work, and I knew she had no relations that
would give her any thing but advice; . . . but what does she do but

shut herself up, work night and day, and give the lie to every one of" the rumors he has spread (RC, 345). Even at this point he plans to trick her out of some of her money; although he is entitled to none of it following the divorce, he assumes that "all women are fools about law matters" (RC, 345). But the intervention of John Perry eliminates Stahle from Gertrude's life—forever, one assumes, given the way all wrongs are righted by the end of Rose Clark.

Gertrude shares with Rose Clark an essential goodness and patience: as Gertrude waits for her ordeal with Stahle to conclude, so Rose waits for Vincent to return. But in her independence and knowledge of the world, Gertrude more nearly resembles Ruth Hall/Fanny Fern, and her analyses of midnineteenth-century society echo those in Fern's newspaper columns of the period. Burned by her experience with Stahle, she has no interest in marrying again and is suspicious of the motives of men who would be interested in marrying her. When John questions her on this point she replies, "there are undoubtedly men in want of housekeepers, and plenty of widowers in want of nurses for their children. My desires do not point that way" (RC, 284). In addition to commenting on gender relationships, Gertrude, like Fanny Fern, is fond of comparing New York and Boston, to the decided advantage of the latter. Although Fern remarked frequently on the stuffiness of Boston "society," she nevertheless found Boston more "civilized" than her adopted New York, and Gertrude shares this view. She extols the democratic openness of Boston Common, whereas in New York it is difficult to find "a stray blade of grass or a fresh blossom" (RC, 369). New York streets are clogged with traffic, whereas Boston features "green, winding lanes" (RC, 370); Boston and its inhabitants seem generally well taken care of: "Do you not see that the gutters are inodorous; that the sidewalks are as clean as a parlor floor; that the children are healthy, and sensibly dressed; that the gentlemen here do not smoke in public; . . . and that there is a general air of substantiality and well-to-do-ativeness pervading the place . . . ?" (RC, 373).

The most obvious way in which Gertrude speaks for Fanny Fern is her sarcastic diatribe against book reviewers, occasioned by Rose's proposal that she "turn authoress" to support herself, and fueled by Fanny Fern's experience with the reviewers of Ruth Hall two years earlier. Book reviewers, according to Gertrude, may be ignorant—"a fellow who knows no difference between a sun-flower and a violet"—or they may be jealous of the author's talent and retaliate with an unfavorable review. An author's work may be attacked merely because she is female, or because she makes fun of something sacred to the reviewer, or because he is prejudiced against American authors. Gertrude's last point bears out Mary Kelley's thesis that it was the public nature of being a successful writer that was most problematic for the women authors of Fanny Fern's generation: "Fame is a great unrest to a true woman's heart. The fret, and tumult, and din of battle are not for her" (*RC*, 291). In warning Rose against entering the public realm, Gertrude underscores her status as the conventional "true woman."

Despite the difference in characterization of their heroines, *Ruth Hall* and *Rose Clark* have structural similarities. As she did in her first novel, Fanny Fern here shifts the locale and the narrative perspective with each new chapter. The chapter in which Gertrude discourses on book reviewers, for example, is followed by a chapter that introduces Madame Vincent's greedy servant, Anne, and three of the chapters of the novel are letters from the poet Finels to a friend (it is in one of these letters that the reader learns of the death of Dolly Howe). But the purpose of these rapid changes in narrative stance is different in the two novels. Whereas in *Ruth Hall* they serve to present the many voices that attempt to define Ruth, and to point up the contrast between social classes, in *Rose Clark* they provide a way for Fanny Fern to keep the various threads of her coincidental narrative all going on at once. Thus Vincent is glimpsed in several chapters on his journey to find Rose, a conversation involving Balch is introduced to tell readers that Mrs. Markham has been fired from the orphanage and prepare for her death in the last chapter, and the author returns the reader to Difftown for Mrs. Bond's peaceful death to show how virtue is rewarded.

Rose Clark represents Fanny Fern's second and last attempt at novel-writing. Thereafter she devoted her energies to her newspaper columns and to writing books for children. Although her second novel had an enthusiastic readership, her increasing interest in social injustice and the ills of a materialistic culture was perhaps best served by the immediacy of her weekly columns. And with the story of Gertrude Dean, she had completed her own autobiography to that point, so that Sara Willis could henceforth be completely subsumed under Fanny Fern.

Chapter Five

"Little Ferns"

Fanny Fern's Books for Children

In a story titled "The Little Dandelion Merchant" in *Little Leaves for Fanny's Little Friends*, Fanny Fern's first of three collections of stories for children, published in 1854, a young boy named Jemmy earns money by picking and selling dandelions for ninepence a basket. When he approaches a house where he hopes to make a sale, knowing that "the old housekeeper and her mistress have both a tooth for dandelions," a snobbish footman kicks Jemmy's basket of greens down the street. Picking up his scattered wares, Jemmy remarks through his tears that "ninepence would have bought my book," whereupon a disembodied voice announces that some kind stranger is giving the boy the book he desires—" 'the fairies have sent it you.' " The moral of the story concerns generosity, as the author intones that "one need not be a 'Rothschild' to make a fellow creature glad."[1]

It is significant that Jemmy's heartfelt desire is for a book, rather than a loaf of bread or a pair of shoes, because the love of books and reading is one way in which Fanny Fern identifies the sympathetic characters in her fiction. Both Rose Clark and her mother, Maria, in Fern's 1856 novel *Rose Clark* value books and reading—and, consequently, education— whereas the less sympathetic characters, such as Mrs. Markham and Rose's Aunt Dolly, dismiss books as frivolous. Given the high value that Fanny Fern placed on children's reading, it is appropriate that children were not just frequent characters in her fiction, but readers of it as well; in addition to *Little Leaves*, she published *The Play-Day Book* in 1857 and *The New Story Book for Children* in 1864.

Nineteenth-Century Children's Literature

In the midnineteenth century, when Fanny Fern wrote her books for children, no lengthy tradition of American children's literature existed; indeed, a separate literature intended for young readers was a relatively recent concept. The development of children's literature, in both England and America, was influenced by religion, by attitudes toward childhood itself, and by the slow growth of the literacy rate before the institution of widespread education in the 1870s. For children in the Puritan colonies, there were explicitly theological tracts for children, such as James Janeway's *A Token for Children* and John Cotton's *Spiritual Milk for Babes*, and well into the nineteenth century, books for children maintained a decidedly didactic tone and purpose. With children alternately regarded as miniature adults and as beings whose natural inclinations toward evil had to be severely restrained, such an emphasis is not surprising. Monica Kiefer, in *American Children through their Books, 1700–1835*, describes the dearth of children's literature in Colonial America: "No period in the history of American juvenile literature is . . . so bleak and uninspiring as the first seventy-five years of the eighteenth century. During this time no real effort was made to provide suitable reading material for the young. Children everywhere were treated not as undeveloped beings but as ignorant men and women, and nothing was written especially for the needs of the immature mind. Instead, little ones were expected to digest as best they could the heavy literary diet of adults."[2] Although abridged versions of such British novels as *Pamela, Clarissa Harlowe, Tom Jones,* and *Gulliver's Travels* were available in the late eighteenth century, the moralistic tone of literature for children persisted until the Civil War era when, in the words of Alice M. Jordan, there was "the first widespread awakening to the need of critical appraisal, the first wholehearted liberality toward children's tastes and interests, admitted without boundary, without propaganda."[3]

In the early decades of the nineteenth century, religious organizations and a generation of English women writers for children kept the emphasis on morality and didacticism. In 1830, the American Sunday School Union decided to foster a literature for children consonant with its own aims—books that children could take home from Sunday school for family reading. In the guidelines for prospective authors can be seen the several strands of religious purpose, a call for a distinctly American literature, and the beginnings of an awareness of the special needs of children: "(1) The book must be clearly and absolutely of a moral and religious character. (2) It must be graded and adapted to the capacity of the growing mind of the child. (3) It must be of a high order of style and fairly good literature. (4) The book must be American and for American children" (Jordan, 24). The effects on children's literature of the American Sunday School Union continued for the next 30 years, finally to be supplanted by the rapid growth of public libraries in the 1870s.

Meanwhile, a group of English writers whose works were immensely popular in America exerted a more secular but equally didactic influence. Written at the turn of the nineteenth century, works for children by these authors, who were termed *utilitarians* and *rationalists*, stressed useful virtues that were valuable for an emerging nation. Maria Edgeworth's *The Parent's Assistant* (1796), Anna Barbauld's *Lessons for Children* (1778), and Sarah K. Trimmer's periodical *The Guardian of Education* (1802–1806) announce in their titles their didactic purposes; more evangelical were works such as Martha Sherwood's *Little Henry and His Bearer* (1814). What all of these authors shared was a conviction that literature for children should be useful rather than fanciful—stories that could teach moral and ethical lessons. They "soundly condemned fairy tales and all nonsense such as Mother Goose rhymes; while in the task of making children upright, generous, and resourceful, they confined themselves to staid tales of exact literal truth" (Kiefer, 18).

The late eighteenth and early nineteenth centuries also saw the development of a series of highly successful periodicals for children, frequently with religious or didactic purposes. The most important of these for their influence on Fanny Fern's writing for children were begun within a year of each other: *The Juvenile Miscellany*, with Lydia Maria Child as its editor, in 1826, and Nathaniel Willis's own *The Youth's Companion* in 1827. *The Youth's Companion* was begun with a decidedly religious orientation, encouraging children to be pious as well as to develop more secular virtues. As time passed, this weekly periodical, on which Sara Willis worked before her first marriage in 1837, became less devout, but, as Alice Jordan puts it, "*The Youth's Companion* kept its definite view as to what was healthy and moral for children, rejecting both love-making and killings as unsuitable" (40). That *The Youth's Companion* endured until late in the nineteenth century owes much to its steady adherence to widespread middle-class values. Mrs. Child's *Juvenile Miscellany*, on the other hand, was ultimately defeated by its editor's outspoken support of unpopular causes—mainly abolition, but also the rights of Native Americans. Carolyn Karcher describes the conflict between Child's roles as author and activist: "As a children's writer, Child embraced the mission of diffusing the morality of the rising middle class among the widest possible audience, thus making it the means of bridging class conflicts in a society where they were beginning to break into the open. As an abolitionist, on the contrary, Child necessarily assumed the burden of stirring controversy on a bitterly divisive issue which the majority of her middle- and upper-class readers wanted at all costs to keep under a lid."[4] Although undisguised pleas for racial harmony were elements of the stories that appeared in the *Miscellany*, it was not until Child issued her abolitionist tract *An Appeal in Favor of that Class of Americans Called Africans* in 1833 that subscribers in large numbers withdrew their support; *The Juvenile Miscellany* was passed to the editorship of Sarah Josepha Hale—best known for editing *Godey's Lady's Book*—in 1834.

Lydia Maria Child was not the only prominent woman writer of the early nineteenth century to write for children, nor was she the only one who espoused a liberal social philosophy. Contributors to *The Juvenile Miscellany* included Lydia Sigourney, Eliza Leslie, and Catharine M. Sedgwick. As Elva S. Smith notes in *The History of Children's Literature*, "clearly, these were women of brains and courage, not mere hack writers or dilettantes, and their books for children were published in numerous editions over a space of many years."[5] In one sense, it is by no means surprising that nineteenth-century writers for children were predominantly women. As mothers, nurses, and governesses, they unquestionably spent more time with children than did most men, and if they did not, may well have felt that they should: Carolyn Karcher speculates that Lydia Maria Child wrote for children as compensation for her "motherless childhood" and "childless adulthood" (68). In addition, as the century progressed, women were increasingly regarded as the guardians of the kind of morality that the majority of children's literature promulgated.

Julia Briggs suggests a more complex and provocative relationship between women writers and nineteenth-century children's literature—a relationship that takes into account the problematic position of women as professional writers and the gradual change in children's literature from the didacticism and moralism of the early century to a post–Civil War literature featuring characters—such as Mark Twain's Tom Sawyer and Huck Finn and Louisa May Alcott's "little women"—who defy or question the rules and stereotypes of good little children: "To chart the association of women writers with children's books for the first hundred and fifty years [the 1740s to the 1890s] is to record the progress by which their authors progressed from giving instruction to an identification with their readers, from proving themselves responsible adults to allowing themselves to adopt the subversive tones of childhood."[6] What Briggs suggests is that as the position of woman as professional author became more acceptable, women were to some extent freed from the necessity to appear as "responsible adults" and therefore able to create children's literature that appealed to the fanciful, imaginative, and mischievous tendencies of childhood. Briggs's theory suggests, in turn, that the development of children's literature in the nineteenth century may have had as much to with evolving perceptions of the women who wrote it as with changes in cultural attitudes toward the needs of children.

Little Ferns

It is difficult to know exactly what motivated Fanny Fern to write books for children, although her love of and high regard for children is clear in the rest of her writing. Also, her first children's book, *Little Ferns for Fanny's Little Friends*, was published just eight years after the death of her eldest child, and by the time her third, *The New Story Book for Children*, was published in 1864, she had adopted her granddaughter, Ethyl, and so was a mother once again. Surely, too, she was to some extent influenced by her work with her father's *The Youth's Companion*, with which she was associated during the eight years between her graduation from Catharine Beecher's academy and her marriage to Charles Eldredge. If Fanny Fern's children's books lack the overtly theological messages of *The Youth's Companion* in its early years, they are nevertheless presided over by a benevolent deity who smiles on good children, and are filled with moral tales and object lessons that are consonant with the didactic nature of children's literature of the period. Indeed, although Fern avoids a narrow piety, and her books often betray her rebellious spirit and strong opinions, they differ little in intent from that announced by Nathaniel Willis in his prospectus for *The Youth's Companion*, "a small weekly journal, which should entertain . . . children and insensibly instruct them; which should occupy leisure hours, and turn them to good account; which should sanction and aid paternal counsel and pulpit admonition; which should, in an easy and familiar manner, warn against the ways of transgression, error and ruin, and allude to those of virtue and piety."[7] In the process of being entertained, then, children would be educated in the ideal values of an emerging middle-class culture, for the purpose of growing into dutiful, contributing citizens. As Anne Mac-Leod points out in *A Moral Tale*, Americans of the period lived with the paradox that the virtues of selflessness, generosity, and cooperation such literature was meant to inculcate were at odds with "much of the social and most of the economic behavior of the society": "The material success so prized by Americans . . . was plainly the reward of activities very different from the ideal behavior of a Christian. The drive for economic success encouraged ambition, aggression, and a competitive spirit."[8]

That Fanny Fern was aware of this paradox is clear in her novels and newspaper columns as well as in her books for children. One of the reasons for her concern with great disparities between socioeconomic levels in America is precisely her perception that those who achieve substantial material comfort have often either done so because of greed or selfishness or have been coarsened by their experience of competition for wealth. In the children's books as in the novels and columns, rural life is preferable to urban, the poor are generally more caring and virtuous than the rich, and the natural is favored over the artificial. (It is worth remembering that although we associate the term *rags to riches* with the novels of Horatio Alger later in the century, his heroes seldom achieve more than a moderately comfortable way of life.) Although Fanny Fern does not resolve the paradox that virtue seems to reside in poverty—that the successful lives promised to children who absorb the lessons of didactic literature could themselves erode the lessons learned—she does seem optimistic about the rewards of hard work. In "The Little Dandelion Merchant," cited earlier, although little Jemmy's sale is foiled by the "pampered footman," he is described as the determined "merchant" of the title: "Jim is a Yankee, (born with a trading bump,)" (*LF*, 59), and his demeanor after his dandelions are spilled is "rebellious" (*LF, 60*). It seems clear that Jemmy will survive and even prosper—and *perhaps* retain from the gift of a book the spirit of generosity.

The stories in *Little Ferns for Fanny's Little Friends* are told by "Aunt Fanny" to her young readers; the same invented *persona* who had become well-known by 1854 in her newspaper columns for adults thus spoke to children as well. In this regard, Fanny Fern was an exception to the rule in children's literature according to which writing as a profession for women was not presented as an option: "Fictional counterparts of many of the authors, that is, women who made a living by writing, rarely appeared in their stories" (MacLeod, 96). "Aunt Fanny" adopts a storytelling voice, frequently anticipating and responding to the reactions of her listeners/readers, but she often presents herself as sitting at a desk, looking out at the streets of New York, as she composes her stories. The voice of Aunt Fanny is in fact that of a doting aunt who wants, as she says in her preface, to "please and divert" her readers while helping them to improve morally. Most of the stories are framed as "true"—scenes that

Aunt Fanny has observed or in which she has been involved, often as a sort of social worker—lecturing a cigar-smoking boy on the evils of tobacco, feeding or giving money to street urchins, and visiting a family of Irish immigrants—thereby serving as a moral exemplar for her readers. The children whom Fanny Fern imagines as her readers are at the very least middle-class. She assumes that they have servants (whom they should treat kindly), that they are well-dressed and well-fed (for which they should be grateful), and that they have doting mothers and fathers (whom they should obey).

Most of the children in *Little Ferns* are not as fortunate as her imagined readers. One pervasive theme of the book is the precariousness of both financial stability and life itself. When fathers die or take to drink, mothers and children are suddenly and invariably reduced to poverty. Many of the characters in the stories who are in straitened circumstances can testify to previous material comfort, cut short by accident, illness, or death. In "A Street-Scene," for example, Rosa Simon's father "lost all his property at once" (for an unspecified reason) and commits suicide, and Mrs. Simon becomes a prostitute—although the word is, of course, never used: she and Rose live in "a house where wicked people dwell, who live by breaking all God's commandments" (*LF*, 174). The father in "Cicely Hunt; or, The Lame Girl" is killed in a duel, which impoverishes his wife and child. In this story, education is the salvation of the family; because Cicely is a good student, she attracts the attention of the wealthy man who killed her father and who has felt remorse ever since. Fanny Fern provides another instance of financial instability in midnineteenth century America in this story. Extolling the virtues of education, saying that it is "worth as much as money in the bank," she continues: "and more, too, because banks often turn out great humbugs, and then people lose all the money they have placed in them" (*LF*, 207).

The uncertainty of financial stability, in addition to reflecting the realities of the time, is also used to press home moral lessons about snobbishness and placing too much importance on material possessions. If a little girl who one day had her own nursemaid the next day lived in a damp cellar, children were warned against smugness and pretention. Given Fanny Fern's dislike of what she called the "fashionables," this was a natural theme for her to pursue. In an early story in *Little Ferns*, subtitled "Who is Rich?—Who is Poor?", Aunt Fanny comforts a little girl who envies a rich girl riding in a carriage by first reminding her that she has all the necessities of life—health, food, and a loving family—and then telling her that the rich little girl is lame and has an uncaring mother. The stated moral of the story is, not surprisingly, "money is not happiness" (*LF*, 19).

If poverty is always just around the corner, so too is death. Mothers die of consumption, fathers die of cholera or despair over financial reverses, and children die from accidents, "brain fever," and sometimes for no apparent reason—especially infants. While the specter of death, like that of financial difficulty, reflects statistical actualities of the time, it, too, is used for didactic ends. The frequency with which children are orphaned in literature for children had several instructional purposes, which Anne McLeod outlines thusly. "The importance of parental love and protection was dramatized by its loss; the importance of parental teaching was demonstrated by how well the orphaned child was able to manage [on] his own. The Christian obligation to practice charity was given point by picturing the desperate straits of an orphaned and helpless child" (60–61). "The Charity Orphans" in *Little Ferns* consists of a dialogue between Aunt Fanny and a friend who finds the sight of a procession of orphans a "pleasant" one. Aunt Fanny disagrees, finding the regimented children a source of "heart-ache"—"full well I know it takes something more than food, shelter and clothing, to make a child happy" (*LF*, 37). As she would later in *Rose Clark*, Fanny Fern insists that nothing less than the love of a family is necessary for a child's well-being.

The deaths of children were commonly used in juvenile fiction to stress the religious tenet that life in heaven is preferable to life on earth. Those who mourn such deaths are consistently reminded that the children have become angels and have gone to live with God. Like other authors of her time, Fanny Fern was sanguine about the potential for the salvation of young souls, but she is quick to point out that the transition from child to angel could be slight consolation for those left behind. Little Kitty, beloved daughter of Tim the shoemaker in the story "Crazy Tim," is run over by a train, whereupon Tim, a widower, loses touch with reality in his grief and is taunted as "crazy Tim" by the town's children. The moral of "Crazy Tim" teaches children to understand people's histories and behavior; presumably, the death of a child close to their own age will be a compelling impetus for them to be kinder to those like Tim. The death of a loved one is used to point up a similar moral in "The New Cook," in which the drowning death of Betsey's husband Tom forces her to go "into service" as a cook. Betsey's loss has made her "one of the nervous sort," making her a target for teasing by the children of the family. When their practical jokes cause her injury, followed by the unbiquitous "brain fever," the children are properly repentant, vowing to "make poor Betsey's lonely life as happy as ever they could" (*LF*, 249). As in "Crazy Tim," the children are not punished for their cruelty; rather, they are instructed by understanding the truth—guilt seems to work better than a spanking.

Not all of Aunt Fanny's instruction in *Little Ferns* is of a moral nature. She is also concerned with building her young readers' vocabularies and understanding of concepts. After using the word *picturesque* in one story, she adds parenthetically "Aunt Fanny knows that's a long word, but you must look it out in the dictionary" (*LF*, 63). Similarly, having used the word *digression*, Aunt Fanny explains: "Do you know what that is? It is leaving off what you are about, to dance off to something else" (*LF*, 210). In addition to the dictionary, Aunt Fanny sends her readers to the atlas. A young hero in one of her stories lives in Chicago, about which she writes, "you will find that place if you look in your Atlas, and I should like to have you find it, because I want you to remember all about this dear little boy" (*LF*, 292). More local places that an atlas would not list, Aunt Fanny identifies in the text. When one of her villains is sent to the Tombs, she parenthetically describes this prison as "a place in New York for such people" (*LF*, 175), and about an "intelligence office"—which we would call an employment agency—she notes that "it's a place where servant girls go, to hear of families who wish to hire help" (*LF*, 250). Occasionally, as in a story titled "Frontier Life," she introduces subjects she believes are remote from her readers' experience: "'Frontier life!' I think I hear my little readers echo, knitting their brows; 'frontier life,—I wish FANNY FERN wouldn't write about things we don't understand.' Suppose I should tell you a story to *make* you understand it? How would you like that?" (*LF*, 141). Although the story of frontier life ends tragically when a young boy dies after getting lost in the woods, Fern stresses the spirit of neighborly cooperation fostered by the wilderness environment.

Another subject on which Aunt Fanny feels she should instruct her young readers is the lives of America's growing immigrant population— primarily the Irish and Italians. With few exceptions, her attitude is one of sympathy for the immigrants' struggles to learn English, find jobs, and work their way out of the cellars and ghettos they inhabit to participate in the promise of the American dream. In "Hetty's Mistake," a little girl learns the value of education when she teaches the family's Irish cook, Bridget, to read and write, and in "New-York in Shadow" she applauds the efforts of a Mr. Pease to provide jobs and education for residents of the infamous Five Points area of New York. The industriousness of immigrants is the subject of several stories in *Little Ferns*. "A Peep Under Ground" takes readers to the cellar home of two Irish families, the Raffertys and the Rourkes, who compete with each other in devising clever ways to feed their families; about the Rourkes' jealousy of Michael Rafferty's successful scheme to make and sell butter, Mrs. Rafferty says, "It was always the way . . . if a body got up in the world, there were plenty of envious spalpeens, sure, to spite them for it" (*LF*, 159). In "All About the Dolans," Bridget Dolan keeps her large brood of children in food and clothes despite a husband who wastes the family's scant resources on smoking and drinking—one of several temperance messages in this collection. Only one immigrant character is cast in the role of villain: the Irish woman in "The Little Tambourine Player" who steals a child and forces her to play the tambourine while the woman begs for money.

Several stories in *Little Ferns* draw upon the same autobiographical material that informs Fanny Fern's novel *Ruth Hall*. Both "Little Floy" and "The Little Martyr" describe briefly periods of hardship followed by improved circumstances due to the industry of a widowed mother. In the former story, Floy recalls earlier, happier years in a house in the country as she lives in poverty in an urban apartment with her mother, abandoned by fair-weather friends. In the end, Floy's mother becomes a successful writer—"has earned plenty of money for herself" (*LF*, 26)—and mother and child are once again happy. "The Little Martyr" tells of a child being sent away to live with a mean grandmother, as Sara Willis had been forced to send Grace to live with the Eldredges, because she cannot support two children. Although this story does not specify the means by which little Nettie's mother achieves financial security, it too has a happy ending, with mother and child reunited.

The final chapter of *Little Ferns for Fanny's Little Friends*, titled "Children in 1853," is a child-advocacy essay—a plea for the rights of children—although it is aimed, as is the rest of the book, at middle-class readers. Fanny Fern is not arguing here for child-labor laws or universal public education; instead, she asks that children be allowed to *be* children and that they be treated and respected as people with feelings. Aunt Fanny's "creed," which, she says, "you may read . . . to your mother if you like," calls for wholesome food, sensible clothing, and school benches with backs on them. Adults are cautioned to keep promises they make to children and to respect their rights to their own property. "Little children," writes Aunt Fanny, are "all that is left us of Paradise" (*LF*, 297–98).

The Play-Day Book

In her preface to her second book for children, *The Play-Day Book: New Stories for Little Folks* (1857), Fanny Fern testifies to the popularity of *Little Ferns for Fanny's Little Friends* by noting that since its publication she has received "many letters, and messages, from little children all over the country asking me 'to write them soon another little book of stories.'" As though to further underscore the popularity of her work, a bookseller on a train in the story "The Journey" has in his stock not only *Fern Leaves from Fanny's Port-folio*, but also "Second Series and Little Ferns, too." When she asks the young bookseller, who does not know she is the author, who wrote *Fern Leaves*, he ponders and then answers "with the air of one who has hit it, 'Fanny's Portfolio, ma'am.'"[9] Fern and her young companion are much amused by the conversation. Also in her preface, Fern explains the title she has chosen for *The Play-Day Book*: "I call it 'The Play-Day Book;' because I made it to read when you are out of school, and want to be amused. If, while you are looking only for amusement, you should happen to find instruction, so much the better." Both children and adults are sure to "find instruction" in *Play-Day*, but the stories are longer and more interesting than those in *Little Ferns*, and the moralism is less heavy-handed, the messages usually more subtle. In the first story in the volume, a mother and daughter have an exchange about what the youngster considers a "good" story; the young girl speaks against overt morality and contrivance: "I hope it is funny, I hope there ain't any 'moral' in it. Katy Smith's mother always puts a moral in; I don't like morals, do you, mother?" (*PD*, 8). Preparing to tell her daughter a story, the mother receives the further instruction that the story should not begin with "Once on a time" nor end with "They lived ever after in peace, and died happily." Upon being presented with these requirements, the mother asks for a bit more time so that she can "fix up" her story, but the daughter responds, "No, mother, that's just what I don't want. I like it best unfixed" (*PD*, 9).

If by "unfixed" the young girl means a story not contrived to convey a moral message or to show virtue rewarded and vice punished, she would be quite disappointed in the stories in *Play-Day*. Although none of them begins with "Once on a time," most of them are designed to make clear statements about values or behavior, ranging from proper pet care to temperance. Several of the stories are intended to show how adults should behave toward children by describing models of good parenting or, alternatively, instances of child neglect. Fanny Fern also introduces in

Play-Day the exemplary tale—a story of the rise to prominence from humble origins of a famous person—which she would use even more extensively in her third children's book in 1864. It is unfortunate, although not surprising, that the book perpetuates a number of racial, ethnic, and gender stereotypes. Although in her writing for adults Fern showed a tendency toward progressive and even radical social thought, the simplification necessary for young readers seems to have pushed her into a similar oversimplification of the characteristics of blacks, the Irish, men and women.

In some ways the most amusing and fanciful stories in *Play-Day* concern the proper care of pet cats. Instead of presenting a child abusing or neglecting a cat and then being suitably punished, she writes from the perspective of the cat, as she had in "Letter from Tom Grimalkin to his Mother" in *Little Ferns*. In "History of a Family of Cats," Mrs. Tabby Grimalkin gives her five kittens to various homes in the neighborhood, and a month later listens to their stories of how they are being treated. As good and bad treatment are being contrasted, the youthful reader learns that cats should be well-fed and should not be abused by children, that catching mice is natural for them, and—perhaps most important—that mother-love extends to the realm of cats. The story "Puss and I" argues for recognizing the natural behavior of cats by proposing that human beings do similar things. When, for example, "Muff" is chastised for putting a paw in the goldfish bowl, she reminds her owner that just that morning she bought a fresh lobster and told her cook to boil it alive—"if you kill creatures for your dinner how should a poor little cat be expected to do better?" (*PD*, 167).

If the stories about cats are amusing, those with temperance as their theme are quite the opposite. Fanny Fern was vehement in her opposition to the use of both tobacco and alcohol, but while the former was a personal annoyance, she saw alcohol as the destroyer of fathers and family livelihoods. Like many other temperance advocates of her time she blamed the problem of drunkenness not on the individual drinker, but on those who sold the "demon rum," and she would likely have been in agreement with the author of a book advertised on the end-papers of *Little Ferns for Fanny's Little Friends: Dick Wilson, The Rumseller's Victim; Or, Humanity pleading for the Maine Law*, billed as a "thrilling temperance tale." After describing a drunken father in the story "The Little Sisters," Aunt Fanny adopts the rhetoric of the temperance tract: "Oh, what could have turned that once kind man into such a cruel brute? Ask him, who, for a few paltry pence, sells the *Rum* that freezes the hearts of so *many* little girls' fathers, and sends their patient, all-enduring mothers weeping to the grave!" (PD, 219).

In "A Temperance Story" she is even more explicit about the blame for drunkenness and its effects. Mr. Colt, a grocer, sells "Jamaica brandy" and "Old Cogniac" [sic] in the days before an organized temperance movement, when "nobody seemed to think the worse of the man who sold such maddening stuff." Even though women recoiled when he entered the church because he had "taken the bread out of the mouths of so many widows and their children, . . . nobody thought the worse of Mr. Colt for taking, for liquor, all the wages which a poor man had been all the week earning, instead of telling the foolish fellow to take it home to his destitute family" (PD, 250). Mr. Colt finally realizes the error of his ways when his own son, having grown up watching men drink liquor, turns to drink himself and is expelled from college.

The message of "A Temperance Story" is thus not just for children who may learn of the evils of drink, but also for adults who have not yet been fully enlisted in the temperance cause. Aunt Fanny's moral tales for adults most frequently concern the neglect of children, either individually within families or as a more general cultural problem. Mr. Colt's exposure of his son to alcohol constitutes a form of such neglect; more commonly, however, the negligent parent is a mother who is too self-absorbed to give her child either love or proper instruction. A case in point is "The Poor-Rich Child," in which little Eddy, left solely in the care of an inattentive servant, dies of croup because she cannot be bothered to wake up to care for him. Aunt Fanny's final words are blunt: "You and I know he was murdered. Died as hundreds of children die every year, of wicked neglect" (PD, 106). If wealthy children such as Eddy are at risk, much more so are poor children who scramble for survival on the streets of cities. The nameless little boy in "The Little Musician," who is considered a "nuisance" when he plays his accordion for pennies, falls off a pier and drowns. Fanny Fern's only consolation in both cases is her belief that the children have found a better life in heaven.

In contrast to the stories that show the dangers children face are the exemplary tales that describe success stories—youngsters who grow up to occupy positions of prominence. In their emphasis on honesty, hard work, and perseverance, these stories prefigure the popular Horatio Alger novels later in the century; the most significant difference is that most of Fanny Fern's stories are about actual people, such as Horace Greeley, whose names might be familiar to her young readers. By demonstrating to her readers that such influential adults were once ordinary children like themselves, Aunt Fanny doubtless intended to inspire them to similar accomplishments—provided, of course, that they were spared drunken fathers and inattentive mothers. Horace Greeley's mother is one of the best to be found in Fanny Fern's work, and the author uses her description of Mrs. Greeley to protest once again the excesses occasioned by the cult of gentility in midnineteenth-century America: "Women in those days were made of better stuff than most of the women of our day. Horace's mother could not have planted potatoes or raked hay, in corsets or a hoop-skirt. She could not have done it had she lived on cake, cordial, pies and confectionery. She could not have done it had she slept in close, heated apartments. She did none of all these foolish things" (*PD*, 257).

With this sensible, exemplary mother in the background, Horace Greeley sets off for the big city, where he finds a job in a printing office, from which he works his way to the editorship of the *New York Tribune*. The youngster in "The Hod-Carrier" rises even further; after much diligence, he is being suggested as a candidate for President of the United States in 1855. Even recent immigrants could participate in the American dream, although the word *lucky* in the title of "A Lucky Irish Boy" suggests that coincidence has as much to do with Johnny's transformation from an illiterate boy to a partner in a business firm as does merit. And indeed he *is* fortunate to land on the doorstep of Mr. Bond, for whom Johnny's good nature and eagerness are a welcome antidote to his wife's neurasthenic behavior.

Despite Fanny Fern's sympathy with the Irish and other immigrants who attempted to become assimilated into American society despite considerable discrimination, in her writing for children in particular she was subject to the stereotypical portrayals of ethnic minorities and women that were characteristic of her era. Her attitude toward blacks—or at least the attitude represented by Aunt Fanny—is a mixture of condescension and support for their rights. In "The Journey," she writes deprecatingly, "I like black people; they are such a merry people, they are so easily made happy, they are so affectionate, they are so neat" (*PD*, 50). Yet in "The Circus," when Aunt Fanny plans to take her daughter Nelly to a circus, she wants to take "black Nanny" as well, but she wonders whether "Pat Smith allows colored people in his circus." If he does not, Fanny vows that she and Nelly will not go either: "if he is such a senseless Pat as that, he may go without three twenty-five cent pieces, that's all, for Nanny likes a little fun as well as if her skin were whiter" (*PD*, 65). The image of Native Americans is far more negative

and would have been frightening to young readers; in the story "Bald
Eagle" in *Little Ferns* and in "The Wild Rose" in *The Play-Day Book*,
Indians steal children from Caucasian families. Both stories end happily,
but the Indians are portrayed as vengeful and untrustworthy.

In gender stereotyping, also, Fanny Fern is a product of her time: boys
are by nature rowdy and thoughtless; men are strong but given to
passions, such as for alcohol; girls are demure and passive; women are the
long-suffering guardians of morality. In "A Story for Boys" Aunt Fanny
admits to being afraid of little boys because of their rambunctious
behavior—splashing mud on ladies' dresses, teasing little girls, running
their sleds into pedestrians. In "Fun and Folly; A Story for Thoughtless
Boys," a boyish prank actually ends in death: thinking it would be fun to
set fire to the straw in "old John's" cart, a pair of boys startle the horse,
so that the cart rolls over John and kills him. Depictions of young girls in
two of the stories in *Play-Day* are surprising in light of Fanny Fern's
attitude toward education for women expressed elsewhere in her work. In
Rose Clark she approves of Rose's hunger for an education, and many of
her sympathetic female characters are identified with books. But in the
story "The Tom-Boy" she echoes those conservative nineteenth-century
theorists who believed that girls and women were not intellectually or
physically strong enough for the rigors of formal education. At her
mother's insistence, little Maria plays less and studies more, "tossing
from side to side in her bed, at night, repeating parts of her grammar and
geography *in her sleep*, and dreaming that she was being punished for not
getting them more perfectly" (*PD*, 121). By the time Maria is 16,
her spine has become crooked from sitting over her desk, but her mother
sends her to a rigorous finishing school, which completes the ruin of her
health: "Poor sick girl, what good does all her Greek and Latin do her
now?" (*PD*, 123).

In "Bessie and her Mother," Fern upholds the conventional notion
that too much reading unfits women for their true mission in life:
running a household. Little Bessie is finally convinced to put away her
books and learn to clean and sew and cook: "Bessie's mother knew that a
woman is always disgusting, no matter how much she knows, or has read,
unless she is neat and tidy in her habits, and that she is *not* worthy the
name of a woman, if she can not take proper care of her house, or is too
indolent, or slovenly to do it," (*PD*, 147).

While there is no doubt truth in Fanny Fern's advice in these stories,
especially considering women's economic dependence upon men, such
messages to children had the effect of contributing to limited aspirations

for young girls. It is only boys who, in Fern's exemplary tales, can go from humble origins to being newspaper editors or presidential candidates.

The New Story Book for Children

Fanny Fern's third and last book for children, *The New Story Book for Children*, is as much *about* the process by which children are instructed as it is intended to instruct them. Both proper and improper education—by parents and in the schools—are her central subjects, approached in various ways, and sometimes she sounds like a schoolteacher herself, as when she writes, "I want you to notice this particularly" to underscore a lesson. Several times she stresses that what she writes in factual, not fancy, as if to insist on its instructional value. Writing of a bad teacher of Robert Burns, for example, she defends herself against those who would insist that stories for children should focus only on the positive: "I suppose it is not treason to admit, even in a children's book, which, by some, is considered a place for tremendous fibbing, that a teacher may occasionally err, as well as his pupil."[10] At another point she invites her readers to double-check her story about Andrew Jackson against her husband's biography of the former President (James Parton's *Life of Andrew Jackson*, published in 1860): "His after-life [after childhood] is better told than I could tell it you, by a man who is now looking over my shoulder, and who says, I have just told you a fib. If you read "Parton's life of Andrew Jackson," however, you will see that I have told the truth," (*SB*, 75).

At one point, Aunt Fanny takes on the role of an advice columnist. In "A Question Answered," she responds to a little girl who has written to ask her to intercede on her behalf with her mother, who forbids the girl to read "tales or stories." After protesting that she does not like to "come between a mother and her own little girl," Fern goes on to defend the value of reading stories, provided that one's lessons and chores have been done.

In lieu of a preface, Fanny Fern begins *The New Story Book* with "A Story about Myself," which is primarily an account of her mother's beneficial influence on her early life. Hers thus becomes the first of a number of exemplary tales in the volume—stories of the upbringing and later fame of such people as Robert Burns, Samuel Johnson, and Lord Byron. In Fanny Fern's pre–Freudian analysis, the influences of early childhood are crucial to one's eventual outcome, and the mother is far more important in this process than is the father. Her views are, of course, cultural rather than psychological and are derived from the "separate spheres" ideology in which the woman inhabits the domestic arena while the man is engaged in public enterprise. Writing about the early death of Charlotte and Emily Brontë's mother, she proposes that this is a greater blow than the death of a father: "It is very dreadful for a child to lose its mother—much worse, I think, than to lose a father; because a father, be he ever so good and kind, *must* be away from his little ones, and cannot, by any possibility, understand their little wants and ways as a mother can" (*SB*, 83–84). And she makes the same point about two less well-known motherless sisters: "for it is only in part that a father, even the kindest, can fill a watchful mother's place;—he, whose business must be out of doors and away" (*SB*, 232). The one point in *The New Story Book* where Fanny Fern takes the mother's influence to what might have been regarded even in her own day as an absurd extreme is when she reports having seen two elderly men quarreling on the street and traces their behavior to early maternal influence: "I am afraid there are two mothers somewhere (may be they are not alive now), who have been sadly to blame; or those two respectable-looking old men would not be here, degrading themselves by a brawling street fight" (*SB*, 128).

Certainly Lord Byron's mother comes in for much of the blame for what Fanny Fern perceives as the poet's shortcomings. She begins "The Little Lord" rather bluntly: "The world says, he had a very bad temper; and the world says his mother had a very bad temper, too" (*SB*, 157). Even though Fern acknowledges that Byron's mother had an unhappy marriage, she nonetheless maintains that "A mother who cannot, or does not, control herself, cannot, of course, control her child" (*SB*, 158). The selfishness and temper tantrums that Fern says characterized Byron's childhood "overspread all his future life" like "a blighting mildew" (*SB*, 159). While Fern cannot deny Byron's prominence as a poet, she is clearly no fan of his work: "His fine poetical talent was not used to bless, or soothe, or instruct his fellow beings. His powers of pleasing were exerted for unworthy purposes, and wasted upon unworthy objects" (*SB*, 163). For all of these reasons she cannot consider Byron a "great man," and she compares the patient labors of unnamed women to his "spurious greatness": "It is put to shame by the quiet heroism of thousands of women, many of whom can neither read, write, nor spell, who toil on by thousands all over our land, facing misery, poverty, wretchedness in every form, with trust in God unwavering to the last moment of life. That's what I call 'greatness'" (*SB*, 163).

The only thoroughly bad example in Fanny Fern's roster of famous people is Lord Chesterfield, whose letters of advice to his son she considers pernicious because they address only superficial matters of deportment rather than encouraging morality and generosity. She finds most outrageous Chesterfield's characterization of women as "only grown up children" (the actual quotation is "children of larger growth"), which leads her to wonder, "had he a mother? I wonder had she whispered a prayer over his cradle? . . . I always ask these questions when men speak disrespectfully of women" (*SB*, 204).

The poet Robert Burns fares better than Byron and Chesterfield in Aunt Fanny's account. The product of excellent parenting, he proves himself to be a bright and studious boy who absorbs the stories and legends he is told, eventually weaving them into his poetry. But poetry, oddly, is his downfall, for "the farmer who stops to write poems over his plough, seldom reaps a harvest to satisfy hungry mouths" (*SB*, 66), and Burns turns to drink to forget his poverty. Thus "The Ploughboy Poet" becomes one of several temperance stories in *The New Story Book*. Lesser faults than drinking can be excuses or tolerated, however. Samuel Johnson's lifelong irritability can be traced to the fact that scrofula disfigured his face, and the otherwise completely admirable Andrew Jackson has the bad habit of swearing "fearfully" (*SB*, 73).

A passage in "Old Hickory" is one of the few reminders that *The New Story Book* was written during the Civil War. Speaking of the debt that Americans owe to those who fought for American independence, she writes in the tone of an outraged Yankee: "Until recently, our houses were not burned down over our heads, or ransacked and robbed, nor our mothers and sisters insulted before our eyes, nor our fathers and brothers dragged off as prisoners of war, and kicked and cuffed for sport by the enemy" (*SB*, 69). Fanny Fern's abolitionist sympathies are quite apparent in her account of John Brown, whose raid on Harper's Ferry, Virginia, in October 1859 was unsuccessful in freeing the slaves of the region but made him a legend to Northern sympathizers. Fern credits Brown's rural upbringing, his early contact with friendly Indians, and especially his witnessing of a slave boy his own age being beaten for his lifelong dedication to the abolition of slavery. As a contributor to the John Brown legend, Fern dwells on the details of his capture, imprisonment, and eventual hanging, and closes by quoting from the popular song that helped to keep his memory alive: "But there is fierce fighting down in Virginia to-day; for, though John Brown's body lies mouldering in the grave, *His soul is marching on!*" (*SB*, 55).

In this, her last book for children, Fanny Fern is at least as concerned to fire the ambitions of her young readers as she is to instill in them the proper moral character to make them good Christian citizens. As in her earlier work, there are warnings about the evils of drink, excessive egotism, and cruelty, but most of the stories have to do with overcoming adversity and temptation to become contributors to society, whether of art, political leadership, or technological advancements. In one story she even shows a young French boy overcoming the disability of deafness. Her motivation becomes overt in her story of "The Inventor of the Locomotive," when she states, "I want every boy who reads this to feel encouraged to try what *he* too can do" (*SB*, 293). In this respect, *The New Story Book for Children* is a transitional work, pointing toward the more entertainment-oriented children's literature that gained ground in the 1870s. When Mary Mapes Dodge became the first editor of *St. Nicholas* magazine in 1873, she declared, "Let there be no sermonizing." Part of Dodge's editorial policy for the children's magazine was "to stimulate their ambitions," but, perhaps conscious of the excesses sanctioned by social Darwinism, she added the caveat, "but along normally progressive lines" (Meigs, 280).

Chapter Six
"A lady whom all the world knows"

Fanny Fern and the *Ledger*

Fanny Fern's 16-year association with the *New York Ledger* got off to an auspicious and highly publicized start. Robert Bonner, pleased that the popular author had signed an exclusive contract to write for his paper, advertised that fact by paying for a full page in the *New York Herald,* which repeated over and over the line, "Fanny Fern writes only for the *Ledger.*" Bonner also made public the fact that his new columnist would be paid the unprecedented sum of $100 per weekly column. Thus began a warm, mutually appreciative relationship between editor and writer that ended only with Fanny Fern's death in 1872. When, in 1868, she wrote Bonner a note reminding him of the length of time they had worked together, he responded with a bonus check—a gesture he repeated each year thereafter, accompanying the check with a message such as the following: "My Dear Fanny:—This is a dark, dull day. If the enclosed check, as an indication of my appreciation of your services, should make the sky brighter in your firmament, I shall feel amply rewarded for having signed it. Yours, Robert Bonner" (*MV,* 66). As thanks for Bonner's generosity and genial leadership, Fanny Fern dedicated her 1868 book *Folly As It Flies* to him, using language that reflected Bonner's ownership of a stable of fine horses: "To my friend Robert Bonner, editor of the New York *Ledger:* For fourteen years, the team of Bonner and Fern, has trotted over the road at 2.40 pace, without a snap of the harness, or a hitch of the wheels.—Plenty of oats, and a skilful [*sic*] rein, the secret."

Robert Bonner's investment in Fanny Fern paid off handsomely for both of them. Readers looked forward to seeing what was on Fanny Fern's mind each week—and not just readers of the *New York Ledger:* the absence of copyright laws meant that other papers, both in this country and abroad, were free to reprint her column at will. Evidence of her wide appeal emerges in the columns themselves in a variety of ways. Her column titled "Come On, MacDuff," collected in *Fresh Leaves* (1857) is a response to an editorial comment in the *New York Evening Mirror* regarding a woman who wishes that paper to publish "a communication containing some strictures on Fanny Fern." The editor has refused to do so, because "why should we 'oblige a lady' whom we do not know, and at the same time disoblige a lady whom all the world knows?" The writer "whom all the world knows" is moved to note that this is not the first woman who has been jealous of her success, citing in particular a "Miss Briar," who "wondered if Mr. Bonner, of the New York *Ledger,* gave Fanny Fern, *who had never been out of sight of America,* $100 a column for her stupid trash, what he would give *her,* Miss Briar, who had crossed the big pond, when *she* touched pen to paper! Fanny Fern, indeed! Humph!" (*FL,* 93–94).

Because of her success, Fanny Fern frequently received manuscripts from aspiring writers, requesting both critiques and assistance in placing them with editors. While willing to help someone with obvious talent, she expressed exasperation with the lack of care some writers took with their manuscripts. In "Literary People," for example, she struggles with the dilemma of what to say to a writer who has sent her an "illegibly written" manuscript. "In the second place, the spelling is woefully at fault. In the third place, the punctuation is altogether missing" (*FF,* 276). Later, in "Literary Aspirants," she reports having received enough such manuscripts that she is considering "a printed circular, embodying the above obvious difficulties in the way of 'literary aspirants,' and mail it on receipt of their epistles." Having instead decided to "once for all" state her views in the pages of the *New York Ledger,* she gives fair warning that "after this, every letter from a 'literary aspirant' *which is misspelled* goes into my waste-paper basket."[1]

Even worse than "literary aspirants" with misspelled manuscripts was the "intolerable nuisance" of those who wrote asking for Fanny Fern's autograph. While she happily responded to such requests from friends or from schoolchildren, she resented people who built collections of the autographs of famous people with an eye to their future monetary value. "How a sane adult, in the rush and hurry and tumult of the maelstrom-life of 1868, can find a moment for such nonsense, or can expect *you* to find a moment for it, is beyond my comprehension." She confesses that she keeps the return postage such correspondents enclose and throws away the requests, just as she once sent to a man who asked for a lock of her hair "a curl clipped from a poodle-dog, which at this moment may be labelled with my name" (*GS*, 203–4).

Sometimes Fanny Fern's mail was more gratifying. In "My First Convert," she reports that a Civil War veteran has written to say that, as a result of her repeated exhortations, he has given up smoking, and is "no longer a slave to that filthy habit." Such success encourages the columnist to launch into another lecture on the evils of smoking, in which she notes that she was not "mollified" when someone sent her a package of "Fanny Fern Tobacco." Having other things named after her—"a little waif of a black baby," "a hand-cart," and "a mud-scow"—is a pleasure, but "tobacco—excuse me!"[2] Fanny Fern's strongly held opinions on a variety of subjects brought her invitations to give public lectures— invitations that she always refused. Although the major reason for her refusal to speak in public no doubt was her desire to protect the private life of Sara Willis Parton, a column included in her last collection, *Caper-Sauce* (1872), lists a number of other more minor—although perhaps half serious—reasons. Not having been good at arithmetic, she reasons, how could she figure out a railroad timetable to get from "Pumpkinville to Turnipville"? How could she predict the weather, and thus know what to wear—a major consideration, because, as she notes here and elsewhere, what a woman lectures about is a "minor consideration" to reporters, who are far more concerned with writing about her appearance. At the conclusion of her list of reasons for not going on the lecture circuit is the fact that her husband does so, and "two of that trade in one family is more than human nature can stagger under" (*CS*, 278–80).

Although Fanny Fern sometimes seemed annoyed by autograph-seekers and other results of her success, she obviously never forgot her years of poverty and struggle, and her sympathy for the underdog and the downtrodden was a central feature of her writing throughout her career. Shortly after she and James Parton moved into the house on Oxford Street in Brooklyn that she had bought with her own earnings in 1856, she wrote a column titled "My Old Ink-Stand and I; or, The First Column in the New House," in which she recalls her first efforts at writing while living in a boardinghouse run by one "hyena-like Mrs. Griffin." Speaking to her inkstand as an old and dear friend, she expresses her satisfaction that hard work and determination have taken her away from the disagreeable Mrs. Griffin: "Well, old Ink-stand, what do you thing [*sic*] of this? Haven't we got well through the woods, hey? A few scratches and bruises we have had, to be sure, but what of that?" Indeed, she gives credit to the "scratches, and bruises" for spurring her on to a successful career as a writer: "every rough word aimed at my quivering ears, was an extra dollar in my purse" (*FL,* 103–5).

The "hundred-dollars-a-column story"

The first piece of writing that Fanny Fern was commissioned by Robert Bonner to contribute to the *New York Ledger* was not one of her "Fern Leaves" columns, but instead a melodramatic novella titled "Fanny Ford; A Story of Everyday Life," which appeared in 10 installments, for each of which she was paid the much-touted $100. In her preface to *Fresh Leaves,* in which "Fanny Ford" is reprinted, Fern writes that she is pleased to present in this volume "the 'hundred-dollars-a-column story,' respecting the remuneration of which, skeptical paragraphists have afforded me so much amusement. (N. B.—My banker and I can afford to laugh!)." Despite its subtitle, "Fanny Ford" depends as heavily on coincidence, pathos, and clear-cut heroes and villains as does her second novel, *Rose Clark.* Young Mary Ford is engaged to marry Percy Lee when Percy is convicted of embezzlement and sent to prison. Heartbroken, Mary lapses into a more or less vegetative state and in this condition marries the wealthy but unprincipled Tom Shaw. Mary dies while giving birth to Fanny, and Mary's mother takes care of the child while virtually a prisoner in Shaw's house.

When Shaw breaks his neck in a drunken fall down the stairs, Fanny and her grandmother move to a small house in the country, where Mrs. Ford ekes out a meager living as a seamstress. The peddler who comes to the house one day is none other Percy Lee, now released from prison and completely rehabilitated. Recognizing in Fanny the features of his lost love, Mary, Percy vows to take care of her after her grandmother dies and sends Fanny to live with two different families while he establishes a solid financial base. By the time Fanny is 17, she and the 36-year-old Percy are engaged to be married. Only one impediment to their happiness remains: a man named John Scraggs, whom Percy had attacked years earlier for impugning Mary's honor, vows to prevent the marriage from taking place, but Scraggs dies of a self-inflicted gunshot wound while scuffling with police outside the church, and with this threat removed, Fanny and Percy can begin to live happily ever after, as the last lines of the story make clear: "There are homes in which Love folds his wings contented *forever* to stay. Such a home had Fanny and Percy" (*FL,* 209).

Despite the melodramatic plot and tone of "Fanny Ford," the novella contains Fanny Fern's commentary on several issues of particular concern to her—notably, proper parenting, which was the subject of many of her stories for children, and prison reform, which became a frequent topic of her newspaper columns. A digression in chapter 8 contrasts two philosophies of childrearing. Two farmers named Pike and Rice, who are irrelevant to the plot of the story, disagree about whether love or punishment is a better incentive to good behavior. Farmer Rice, who obviously speaks for Fanny Fern, chides his neighbor Pike for "allers scolding" his son: "I tell you, Pike, it is enough to discourage any lad, such a constant growling and pecking" (*FL,* 149). When Pike calls Rice's ideas "modern notions" and cites the biblical injunction that children should obey their parents, Rice counters with another biblical passage: "Parents provoke not your children to anger, lest they be discouraged" (*FL,* 149–50).

The description of Bluff Hill penitentiary in chapter 5 is occasioned by Percy Lee's incarceration there, but the narrator takes the opportunity to launch an appeal for more humane conditions for prison inmates. Citing bad food, poor ventilation, and cruel methods of punishment, she ends with an exhortation: "Heaven speed the day when the legislative heart, pitiful as God's, shall temper this sword of justice with more mercy" (*FL,* 136).

Advice Columnist

The "hundred-dollars-a-column story" of Fanny Ford ran in the *New York Ledger* in the summer of 1855, and when it concluded Fanny Fern turned to writing the columns that had become her trademark, leaving serialized fiction behind to comment on issues that claimed her notice. In the process, she created a recognizable *persona* that her readers came to know—a woman who thought breakfast was the most important meal of the day, who loved children and hated tobacco in all its forms, who believed in the value of physical exercise, who loved order and despised chaos, and who was married to a biographer. The breezy, conversational style of her columns—in sharp contrast to the conventional melodrama of a story such as "Fanny Ford"—gave them an immediacy that enhanced the sincerity of the author's voice.

Several times Fanny Fern becomes explicit about her reasons for writing. Once, contemplating the grave of an author, she notes that her purpose is to shout "*Courage! Courage!*—to earth's down-trodden and weary-hearted" (*FL,* 237). In a more crusading mood, having witnessed a female clerk being abused by her employer, she announces that she wishes to bring about reforms: "You wonder if you were to sit down and write about this evil, if it would deter even one employer from such brutality to the shop girls in his employ" (*FF*, 194). The result of these motives was to make Fanny Fern a combination of advice columnist, gadfly, and social reformer, and as "Fern Leaves" developed into the 1860s and early 1870s, she became more secure in her convictions and more outspoken. Fanny Fern was amused by the physical images of her that were conjured in readers' minds; in a piece titled "Some Gossip About Myself," she reports that a stranger who called at her house one New Year's Day was surprised by the Fanny Fern he found there: "Well, now, I *am* agreeable disappointed! I thought from the way you *writ*, that you were a great six-footer of a woman, with snapping black eyes and a big waist, and I *am* pleased to find you looking so soft and so feminine" (*GS*, 186–87).

As a giver of advice, Fanny Fern's hallmarks are moderation and common sense—what Marietta Holley, whose career began about the time that Fern's ended in the early 1870s, would call *megum* (medium). Although she believed in hard work, for example, she also believed that women often worked too hard and urged them to find time for themselves and to take their children outdoors. She deplored excesses of any kind, including the following of fads in dress and the punishment of criminals. She adopted the voice of reason and believed that her readers were reasonable enough to take heed; in this respect, she anticipated advice columnists such as Ann Landers and Abigail van Buren. In an amusing sketch titled "Breakfast at the Paxes,'" a woman complains about her husband monopolizing the morning paper and decides to write an article about just such behavior for the *Weekly Monopolizer* so that her husband will see it (*FL*, 67). Although Fanny Fern seldom printed actual letters from her readers, she frequently responds as though to particular individuals, such as "Mary M." in "A Question, and its Answer." Mary's question is whether she should marry an "old bachelor," and Fanny Fern's response is an unequivocal "Don't do it," because the bachelor will be too set in his ways—"as unbending as a church-steeple" (*FL*, 284). On other occasions she addresses her advice to categories of people rather than to individuals, as she does in "To Young Girls." In this column, she advises girls not to mistake adolescent flirtations for long-term commitments, lest they marry too young to complete their educations, thereby becoming dull wives. In a postscript to her column, Fern warns her young readers against accepting presents from men who are not relatives or fiancés, lest their reputations be tarnished. In a rare tone of severity, she verbally shakes her finger in her readers' faces: *"Don't do it, girls"* (FF, 247).

Although Fanny Fern readily adopted the role of counselor to readers of her column, she was vehemently opposed to another kind of advice available to them: the conduct manuals for women that proliferated as the nineteenth century progressed. She especially singled out for criticism the books instructing young wives on how to please their husbands, believing that such books encouraged subservient behavior on the part of women and also that successful marriages required the efforts of husbands as well as wives. Sometimes she is content to deal with such guides in a moment of sarcasm, as in "A Business Man's Home," in which Mrs. Wade, having been so bold as to disagree with her husband, is found "blushing the next moment that she had so far departed from 'The Married Woman's Guide' as to question an opinion which her husband had endorsed" (FL, 12–13). But Fern was capable of being much more blunt in her opposition to manuals for women's behavior. In "Moral Molasses; or, Too Sweet by Half," she calls the "Guide to Young Wives" "the most thorough emetic I know of." Such guides assume, she continues, that "when things go wrong, a wife had only to fly up stairs, read a chapter in the "Young Wife's Guide," supposed to be suited to her complaint, and then go down stairs and apply the worthless plaster to the matrimonial sore," (FL, 210). What most annoyed Fanny Fern about this genre of advice literature was that it offered instruction to women, but not to men. Advice to young girls, for example, teaches them to "always be on hand to mend rips in their brothers' gloves and tempers, and coddle them generally," but she has yet to see the book "which enjoins upon brothers to be chivalric and courteous and gentlemanly to their sisters" (CS, 285).

Much of the advice in the "Fern Leaves" columns is addressed to the institution of marriage, and Fanny Fern is evenhanded in her analyses of marital discord; if men had a tendency to be grumpy and neglectful, women were inclined to be frivolous or bad housekeepers. Both husbands and wives were responsible for the smooth running of both household and marriage. Men had a right to properly cooked food, and women had a right to their husbands' help with childrearing; neither should bear the sole responsibility for family life. The columnist's fairness in her marital advice is reflected in a pair of columns, one directed to "gentlemen" and one to "ladies," in which she describes various kinds of men and women who have no "call" to matrimony—who have unrealistic expectations or improper motivations for marriage. She points to a man who has "wasted his youth in excesses" and who then seeks a "virtuous young girl" to "nurse up his damaged constitution" as a bad candidate for marriage, and similarly characterizes a man who would abandon an invalid wife. Lesser sins may also disqualify a man from the matrimonial roster: retreating behind a newspaper, sitting on his wife's bonnet, or having his beard shaved off. Women are disqualified for neglecting their children, serving bad food, flirting with other men, or coveting their neighbors' finery (*FL,* 107–8).

In "A Discourse Upon Husbands," Fanny Fern adopts a stern tone as she speaks to husbands about several behaviors that make women unhappy. She soundly castigates men who have no kind words for their wives, who are jealous of the attention their wives pay to infants, and who take no responsibility for helping to make a marriage work. It takes, Fern insists, "two years for a young married couple to adjust themselves to their new position," and, perhaps thinking of her in-laws' interference in her marriage to Charles Eldredge, she advises, "Mind that *you* both pull together; shut down outside interference, which is the cause of two-thirds of the unhappiness of the newly married, and you will be certain to do well enough, *at last*" (*FF,* 16–17). In a more amusing vein is "The Last Bachelor Hours of Tom Pax," in which a young man about to be married writes a "last will and testament" to his bachelor days, giving the playthings of the single state—his punch bowl, yellow-covered novels, and cigars—to friends, so that they will not interfere with his marriage (*FL,* 220–22). The sketch acquires a deeper resonance when one notes the date of Tom Pax's will, January 12, 1856—the month and year that Sara Willis married James Parton, who was 11 years her junior. Also in an amusing tone is the column titled "Awe-ful Thoughts," in which Fern takes issue with the assertion that "*awe* . . . is the most delicious feeling a wife can have toward her husband." She wonders how awe could possibly survive in the daily intimacies of marriage, how a woman could be in awe of a man "whose dressing-gown you have worn while combing your hair," and "whom have seen asleep with his mouth wide open!" (*FL,* 107–8).

Religion and Fashion

Two topics that are pervasive in Fanny Fern's fiction and nonfiction writing are religion and fashion, and her goal in addressing both is to urge moderation, humanity, and common sense. Her distaste for orthodox Calvinism, with its wrathful God and fears of eternal damnation, goes back to her childhood experiences with religion; her dislike of high fashion is part of her critique of the "cult of gentility." In a column collected in the volume *Folly As It Flies,* she pauses to register her disgust with the word *genteel* and all that it implies: "Now if there is one word in the English language that I hate more than another, it is the word *genteel.* . . . It is the universal and never-failing indorser [*sic*] of every sham ever foisted upon degraded human nature. . . . [People should resist] the bad example constantly set them by the moneyed class in this country, who are servilely and snobbishly bent on aping all the aristocratic absurdities of the old country," (*FF,* 109–111). Sometimes religion and fashion converge as topics in Fanny Fern's columns, as when people go to church primarily to show off their clothes or when parishioners gossip about the wardrobe of the minister's wife.

The Reverend Payson, from whom Sara Willis received her middle name, had a lasting influence on her attitudes toward religion and the role of ministers; in a household that frequently had ministers as guests, Payson was the only one who spoke of a loving God, and Fanny Fern argued throughout her career as a writer that religion should teach love rather than fear and should minister directly to the needs of people. In her column "Justice for Ministers," she recalls her childhood experience, noting that the bounty of the natural world turned her away from those who called her "a child of wrath": "no bugaboo of anybody's raising could have made me believe that I was born by him to be tormented" (*GS,* 139). Years later, in "Sunday in the Village," she contrasts the sermons of two ministers: a small-town New England preacher concerned with sin and damnation, and a New York minister filled with the love of God. The former is one of many ministers whom Fern characterizes as more interested in doctrine than in the lives of their congregations, and her description helps to define what was for her the ideal religious observance: "I want to know *how to live;* and the Rev.————— only tells me that I've 'got to die.' I want to know how to manage with *to-day;* and the Rev.————— only speculates about what may or what may not be in eternity. I want to be soothed, and helped, and propped, and comforted; and the Rev.————— tries to scare me with an 'angry God' and a 'sure damnation'" (*GS,* 216).

Given her own childhood experiences, Fanny Fern was especially concerned about the way in which religious leaders approached children. The Reverend Paysons of the world were rare, she believed; more commonly, children were taught to fear God and dread Sundays. In "And

Ye Shall Call the Sabbath a Delight," she reports witnessing an afternoon Sunday school in which more than 100 children were packed into a poorly ventilated church to be preached at by a "well-meaning but stupidest of possible ministers." Such forced exposure to drily presented Christianity, she feels, will do far more harm than good: "One hundred and fifty little children to carry away with them from that church (not only for that afternoon, but for a long life of Sundays), a disgust of that blessed day, and what *should* be its sweet and holy services" (*FL,* 91–92). Fern's own recommendations for introducing young children to the Sabbath are contained in the column "What Shall We Do for the Little Children on Sunday?" For very small children, she proposes, church attendance is not a good idea; instead, children should be encouraged to see Sundays as special, pleasant times—"the *cheerfullest* day of all the week"—featuring outdoor walks and special treats (*GS,* 34–36).

Although she maintained a strong belief in God throughout her life, Fanny Fern also believed that people should take responsibility for themselves rather than assigning all good or ill fortune to the will of God. In the spirit of self-reliance of her era, she stated often that waiting for the intervention of God or Providence revealed a lack of normal human ambition. Regarding the admonition to "bide the Lord's time," she is characteristically huffy: "If there is one piece of advice more bandied about by irresolution, imbecility, and moral cowardice than this, I should be glad to know it. As *I* take it, the Lord's time is the first chance you get" (*GS,* 300). Even Providence, she writes, is a "convenient scapegoat for all the human stupidity extant," and "a convenient theology for bad cooks, for unwise school-teachers, for selfish, careless, ignorant parents!" (*CS,* 72). Like Thoreau, Fern wrote to "wake her neighbors up" to their own follies and potential.

One of the greatest human follies that Fanny Fern deplored was the slavish following of fashions in clothing, which became a metaphor for all forms of social climbing in both her fiction and her nonfiction. Although she views men as well as woman as slaves to fashion—men who wear stiff collars, she notes, look like "choked chickens" (*FL,* 249)—she reserves her greatest scorn for women, such as the one she describes in mock-biblical tones in "Knickerbocker and Tri-Mountain": "The New York woman never appeareth without a dress-hat and flounces, though the time be nine o'clock in the morning, and her destination the grocer's, to order some superfine tea. She delighteth in embroidered petticoats, which she liberally displayeth to curious bipeds of the opposite sex. She turneth up her nose at a delaine [woolen muslin], wipeth up the pavement with a thousand-dollar silk, and believeth point-lace collars and handkerchiefs essential to salvation" (*FL,* 98).

It is not only upper-class women, who can afford silk and lace, who are affected by the fashion mania. The "dress furore," she writes, "infects every class and circle," and she is saddened to see young working girls and wives of laborers spending their scant resources on flimsy flounces rather than on sturdy, sensible clothing (*FL,* 295–97). Even immigrant women working as servants are susceptible to the fashion virus. In "Bridget as She Was, and Bridget as She Is," a young girl fresh off the ship from Ireland abandons her sensible dress and shoes for the flimsy, flashy clothing she sees around her; in place of her "dew-defying brogans," she squeezes her "crucified toes" into "narrow, paper-soled, fashionable, high-heeled gaiters" (*FF,* 103–5).

Fanny Fern's concern about the following of fashions in clothing stems not only from her resistance to social climbing; she was an early advocate of clothing reform for the sake of health. Bridget's "crucified toes" are not merely painful—they also prevent her from walking for the exercise that a healthy body needs, just as tightly laced corsets prevent women from breathing properly. Sensible clothes are difficult to find, she complains in "A Glance at a Chameleon Subject": "You should go into the 'furnishing stores for ladies' and children's garments,' and see how *impossible* it is to find *plain, substantial* articles of clothing for *either*" (*FL,* 296). She found particularly pernicious the wearing of hoop skirts by little girls, "whose antelope motions are thus circumscribed, their graceful limbs hidden, and their gleeful spirits checked." The artificiality of hoops and corsets rouses her to a dramatic flourish at the end of "Fair Play": "I affirm that any woman who has not faith enough in her Maker's taste and wisdom, to prefer her own bones to a whale's, deserves the fate of Jonah—minus the ejectment" (*FL,* 304). Watching ice skaters in Central Park, Fern marvels that women can skate at all, with "all that mass of dry goods strung round their waists." But challenged to design a different skating costume for women, she identifies the real obstacle to clothing reform: men. "It is brave *talking,* I know, but the time has not yet come when men, by refraining from rude remarks on a female pioneer in such a cause, would remove one of the chief obstacles to its advancement" (*CS,* 61–62).

Social Reformer

Despite her conventional attitudes toward the sanctity of the family and the consolation of religious belief, Fanny Fern increasingly sounded the note of social reform in her "Fern Leaves" columns. From prisons to diet, race relations to funeral practices, she repeatedly called attention to inhumane and senseless practices and institutions. Although she seldom proposed detailed plans for rectifying the ills she identified, she felt it her duty to point out to readers of the *New York Ledger* problems that threatened the well-being of society, and to read her last four collections of newspaper columns is to gain insight into some of the dilemmas confronting residents of the urban Northeast in the 1860s and 1870s. Some problems, such as muddy city streets, the discomforts of train travel, the difficulty of finding good servants, and organ-grinders who insisted on playing under one's window, she accepted as mere annoyances, but others, she felt, were dangers that concerted effort could alleviate.

The prison conditions that Fern describes in "Fanny Ford" were based on visits she made to Blackwell's Island and the Massachusetts State Prison, both of which she details in her columns. In terms that are remarkably similar to twentieth-century debates about the criminal justice system, she asserts that merely locking up someone has little rehabilitating effect: "I hate the bolts and bars, and I say this is *not* the way to make bad men good." She also proposes some sort of halfway house to help the former prisoner adjust to freedom—"a noble institution where he can find a *kind* welcome and *instant* employment; before temptation, joining hands with his necessities, plunge him again headlong into the gulf of sin" (*CS*, 30–31). When Fern turns her attention to women prisoners on Blackwell's Island, she tells "Mrs. Grundy" to get out of her way. Those who would dismiss these women for their sin against society (which, in Fanny Fern's veiled language, is prostitution) are contemptible enough, but worse in her view are men who view such women as "a necessary evil" to protect "pure" women. Of the sexual double standard, she writes with an air of finality, "The great Law-giver made no distinction of sex, as far as I can find out, when he promulgated the seventh commandment, nor should we" (*CS*, 36). Given the prison conditions she has witnessed, Fanny Fern is happy to report in "Give the Convicts a Chance" that the Massachusetts State Prison has instituted evening lectures for the prisoners. "Surely as God lives," she concludes, "there is a window in the soul of every debased man and woman, at which Love and Mercy may knock and whisper, and be heard" (*FF*, 132).

The schools that Fern describes in her columns about education have a good deal in common with the prisons she visited. In her opinion, school hours were too long, children did not get enough exercise, and they were given academic tasks that were beyond their abilities. As with her other efforts at reform, her central message about education is moderation: a balance between study and play and a sensible diet for growing bodies. In "A Word to Parents and Teachers," she addresses these points with vehemence: "It is pitiful, this dwarfing of American children with improper food, want of exercise, and corkscrew clothes. It is inhuman to require of their enfeebled minds and bodies, in ill-ventilated school-rooms, tasks which the most vigorous child should never have imposed upon his tender years. As if a child's physique were not of the first importance!—as if all the learning in the world could not be put to any practical use by an enfeebled body!" (*FL*, 109).

One of the "tasks" that Fanny Fern frequently singles out for her disapproval is the writing of compositions, a position that seems ironic in light of her own success with essay writing at Catharine Beecher's school. In "Writing 'Compositions,'" she does acknowledge that " 'Composition Day' . . . was only a delight to me," but she is sympathetic with the young girl who writes to her for assistance with a composition. Fern's concern is that teachers assign lofty topics of which children have little knowledge ("your minister might just as well be asked to write a dissertation on French millinery"), and encourage lofty, inflated language rather than clear prose. The result, of which Fanny Fern has direct evidence, is sometimes plagiarism: a school principal has sent her a prizewinning essay that was copied out of one of her own books. The writing of compositions, she concludes, should be "a delight, instead of a bore and a cheat" (*CS*, 168–72).

Proper diet was not an issue that concerned only children. Fanny Fern believed that women, in particular, owed it to themselves and their families to be as healthy as possible, and she frequently railed against the consumption of sweets by "fashionable" women. As an advocate of exercise, sensible clothing, and nutritious food (which in her day in-volved beefsteak and eggs for breakfast), she looked askance at what she termed "the marvellous amount of invalidism among our girls and women" (*CS*, 67) and was convinced that better habits would cure it. In "The Sin of Being Sick," as in other columns, she (though a coffee drinker herself) particularly condemns the drinking of tea, which she terms the *woman's dram*. "I should like," she writes, "to see [a tea-drinking woman] having any 'career,' except fitting herself speedily for a lunatic asylum" (*CS*, 65). As the word *dram* suggests, she considered tea-drinking a form of inebriation: "the drunkards on tea are just as surely sapping the foundations of life, as the devourers of whiskey or gin." Unlike the eating of sweets, the drinking of tea is especially the province of working girls who live in boardinghouses with bad food, and so rely on tea to "set them up" (*GS*, 268). As much an evil as tea is bad bread, which Fern is herself subjected to when she stays at hotels and boardinghouses on her trips to New England. In "Country Diet," she calls for "Home Missionaries having for an object the extermination of the unhealthy and *immoral* bread of New England" (*GS*, 268). However unscientific Fanny Fern's nutritional theories may have been, she somehow knew that sour bread, pastry made with lard, and fried meat did not contribute to the health of the nation.

Despite Fanny Fern's frequent preoccupation with illness and death, she was not in the least sentimental about funerals. Long before Jessica Mitford wrote *The American Way of Death*, Fern castigated the funeral business for promoting showy, expensive funerals that could impoverish a family. She dislikes what she regards as the ghoulish practice of displaying coffins in shop windows "between a millinery establishment and an oyster saloon" and dislikes even more the way undertakers take advantage of the grief-stricken: "The jolly undertaker rubs his hands, for death is busy and business is brisk." The carriages hired for the friends of the deceased to ride to the cemetery, she maintains, "swallow up the little legacy left for the living, by the dead for whom you profess to grieve!" (*FL*, 278–81). The wearing of mourning she also finds unnecessarily ostentatious and expensive, and she understands the social-climbing public well enough to know that the upper class will have to take the lead in abandoning the practice: "I wish that a few sensible, intelligent, *wealthy* people would cease draping and festooning themselves like engine-houses, when a death occurs in a family. I use [the] word '*wealthy*' advisedly; because it is only that class who can really effect a reformation, for the reason that *they* will not be supposed unable 'to pay a proper respect,' as the phrase runs, to the deceased" (*GS*, 41). She particularly deplores the practice of dressing children in mourning: "Is it Christian or even humane, so to surround them with gloom that 'death' shall be a never-ceasing nightmare?" (*GS*, 42). She recommends the adoption of the military practice of wearing black arm bands.

Although Fanny Fern wrote her *New York Ledger* columns during and immediately after the Civil War, and although her abolitionist sympathies are clear, she did not often write directly about the war. Her columns were political in a more indirect way, and she was less concerned with battlefields and generals than she was with individual sacrifice and heroism. She continued to harbor a deep distaste for the South, writing at one point, "The farther a New Englander goes South, the gladder he is to return. . . . In Virginia the grass is too lazy to grow" (*FF*, 148). And she crows unabashedly at the Union victory, which has abolished "the monster slavery" (*FF*, 153). But it is the war on a human level that most interested her. In "The History of Our Late War," she tells of the man who rowed her boat during a summer vacation, who had been imprisoned at Andersonville and narrowly escaped. He is not bitter toward his former enemies despite this experience, commenting that *"they* thought they were as right as we, and they *did* fight well" (*GS*, 123). The "Unwritten History of the War," as one of her columns is titled, is the history of the common soldier, and she is particularly impressed by a display of letters written by soldiers—one of whom held the pencil in his mouth because his hands had been injured. "How often I think of these 'privates,' as they are called, when grand 'receptions' and 'balls' are in progress for some great 'General' in our midst" (*FF*, 162). Fern at one point makes special reference to the "fine soldierly appearance of our colored troops," noting the special interest they had in the success of the Union Forces (*FF*, 147).

The "Woman Question"

By far the most frequent subject of Fanny Fern's reforming zeal was women's rights. She belonged to no organized suffrage group, nor did she go on the lecture circuit, but her newspaper columns again and again argue for more freedom, respect, and better treatment for women in both the public and the private arenas. This is not to say, however, that she was an uncritical champion of her sex; indeed, she believed that women were often responsible for their own problems. The most comprehensive critique of women's bad habits is bluntly titled, "Women and Some of Their Mistakes." In addition to the ubiquitous chasing after fashion, women's "mistakes" include raising their sons to be indolent, speaking in an affected manner, entertaining lavishly instead of simply, and making themselves ill with poor diets—in short, failing to live sensibly and with moderation. At the end of the column, Fanny Fern proposes herself as a model of common sense, noting that she is 55 years old and feels "half the time as if I were just made." "To be sure," she continues, "I was born in Maine, where the timber and the human race last; but I do not eat pastry, nor candy, nor ice-cream. I do not drink tea! I walk, not ride" (*FF*, 87). More amusing but equally straightforward is the columnist's rendition of "Some Varieties of Women." The "rabbit woman" has "four chins and twelve babies"; the "prim woman" has "her mouth always in a prepared state to whistle"; the "butterfly woman" thinks only of her appearance; the "library woman" is "steeped in folios"; and the "female viper" is "all claws, nails, and tongue" (*FF*, 288-89).

Despite these indictments of certain kinds of women, Fanny Fern felt that the majority of women deserved greater respect and admiration for the quiet heroism of their lives. In fact, in "A Gauntlet for the Men" she maintains that "all the heroism of the present day is to be found among women." She refuses to acknowledge that women are the "weaker sex," citing the unrewarded drudgery of wives and mothers, and declaring that "most of the young men of the present day are selfish to the backbone" (*FL*, 286–88). She expresses great annoyance at being asked why women are "so discontented with their lot," answering that "the root of all this discontent is the prevailing physical inability of women to face the inevitable cares and duties of married life" (*FF*, 50–51). She compares the selection of a wife to the selection of a horse, noting that if a man chooses an "ornamental" horse rather than a "working animal," he would naturally select a "*light weight*" carriage for it to pull. (*FF*, 51).

For the plight of the overworked woman, Fern proposes three solutions. The first is simply for women to stop and rest when they are tired; "the world will keep on going round just the same, as if you were spinning a spasmodic tee-totum, as hens do, long after their heads have been cut off" (*FF*, 59). The second remedy is for women to write as an outlet for frustration: "It is not *safe* for the women of 1868 to shut down so much that cries out for sympathy and expression" (*FF*, 62). The most sweeping change that Fern urges in "Women and Their Discontents" is female suffrage, a "lever of power" that can lift women out of their "wretched condition" (*FF*, 66).

As much as Fanny Fern championed marriage and family life, she was well-aware that the wedding ceremony did not ensure that a couple would live "happily ever after." Her own marriage to Samuel Farrington and her observations of the lives around her had taught her otherwise. While women certainly had their faults as wives, Fern saw their shortcomings as relatively minor and uncommon compared to the ways in which husbands could ruin marriages. In "Delightful Men" she explores two of these: men who are charming at social gatherings but rude at home and those who are attracted to one sort of woman but try to make her into a different sort after marriage. The first may say "allow me to differ" when in public, but to his wife at home he says, "Pshaw! what do *you* know about it?" To men who believe this is just a "little thing" she responds that such "little things" are "the hinges of the universe" (*GS,* 45–46). Equally culpable is the man who marries a woman "of marked individuality of character" and subsequently refuses to allow her to disagree with him (*GS,* 50–51). In "Blue Monday" she again addresses men who make unkind remarks to their wives and then wonder why they are upset, using a rather outrageous metaphor: "You are elephants trying with your huge paws to pat humming-birds" (*GS,* 69). Such treatment amounts in Fern's view to "legal murder" of a woman's spirit (*GS,* 70).

The "Fern Leaves" columns address physical as well as emotional abuse. In "Woman's Millennium" the author responds with delight to the news that a judge in Springfield, Massachusetts, has granted a divorce to a woman whose husband beat her, and, further, has announced that he will so decide in all such cases. Fern urges all women with bruises to "emigrate forthwith to this enlightened state" where justice exists: "Here's a man who is *just* to a woman. Think of the rarity of the thing! Compliments, and flattery, and gifts we can all have, till we get to be old women, and some of us afterwards; but *justice,* messieurs! ah! that's quite another thing" (*GS,* 81). Although the judge's decision may be a "rarity," Fanny Fern is nonetheless optimistic about the future for women, believing that "woman's millennium is to come out of all this unquiet and chaos" (*GS,* 83). (She was equally optimistic about women gaining the right to vote, writing in 1868 that "it is only a question of time; that's one comfort" [*FF,* 67]—it was a "comfort" that was to last for more than 50 years.) Yet if progress was being made in America, she could not say the same of England, which she terms "the land, *par excellence,* of wife-beating," and where "John Bull" has a "horror" of "the English female who asserts her right to individuality, in action and opinion, equally with her husband" (*GS,* 90, 87). Fanny Fern's prescription for marital harmony is essentially the Golden Rule, and she asks men to ask themselves the following questions: "*Should I be willing to endure what I expect my wife to bear, were I a woman and a wife?* If not—is it just, or right, or manly, then, for me to expect it of her?" (*GS,* 92).

During the last decade or so of her life, Fanny Fern's columns increasingly defended women's right to be autonomous—to rely upon themselves rather than upon men. She resisted the metaphor of the sturdy oak and the clinging vine: "This 'vine and oak' style of talk is getting monotonous. There is more 'oak' to the women of to-day than there was to those of the past" (*CS,* 297). On the issue of whether women should be allowed to attend concerts and the theater without male escorts, she finds it "cruel" that intelligent women should have to stay home "because

custom did not permit their attendance, unless they could lasso a coat
and hat to bear them company" (*GS,* 282). No longer, she prophesied,
would marriage be a necessity for women: "In my opinion, the 'coming'
woman's Alpha and Omega will not be matrimony. She will not of
necessity sour into a pink-nosed old maid, or throw herself at any rickety
old shell of humanity, whose clothes are as much out of repair as his
morals. No, the future man will have to 'step lively;' this wife is not to be
had for the whistling" (*FF,* 264).

Anticipating one of the central themes of Marietta Holley's *My
Opinions and Betsey Bobbet's,* published a few years later, she foresees an end
to the clinging vine: "Thick-soled boots and skating are coming in, and
'nerves,' novels and sentiment (by consequence).are going out" (*FF,*
265). In "The Old Maid of the Period" she announces the demise of the
negative stereotype of the single woman. The *new* "old maid" does not
"keep a cat, or a snuff-box, or go to bed at dark, . . . nor scowl at little
children, or gather catnip, or apply a broomstick to astonished dogs"
(*GS,* 146). Fanny Fern's old maid is attractive and sensibly dressed; she
goes to parties and concerts, and supports herself as a teacher, lecturer,
writer, or bookkeeper. She "couldn't tell a snuff-box from a patent reaper,
and has a bank-book and dividends: yes, sir! . . . and Woman's Rights
has done it" (*GS,* 148).

But not everyone shared Fanny Fern's support for and optimism about
women's freedom to pursue careers rather than husbands. The impetus
for her column "Women on the Platform" was an article in the *New York
Tribune* about a female theology student who had received two offers of
lectureships. While praising the young woman's accomplishments, the
Tribune writer expressed his hope that if she were to receive an offer of
marriage, she would accept it instead. Fanny Fern disagrees strongly
with the *Tribune,* predicting that the money the young woman earns will
be turned over to her husband, who will dole out to her small amounts of
it for household expenses. "No, Mr. *Tribune,* I differ from you entirely. I
advise no woman to refuse twelve hundred independent dollars a year for
good, honest labor, to become such a serf as this" (*GS,* 112).

Her own refusal to give public lectures notwithstanding, Fanny Fern
argued in favor of women's right to speak in public—and to have any
careers they chose, although she was skeptical of women as doctors. Thus
she was quite annoyed by a speaker who adhered rigidly to the "separate
spheres" ideology, mentioning "with utter contempt" all jobs for
women except housekeeping, and "averring that the education and
training of children were the only things worthy their notice." What

concerns Fern most about this speaker is that he does not mention the *father's* responsibility for the education of children: "Not a word did he say on this head, no more than as if these things were not binding equally on him as on the wife" (*CS, 295–96*). In response to those who opposed women lecturers, she challenges the concept of marriage as women's only means of economic support: "Is [lecturing] less commendable than marrying somebody—anybody—for the sake of being supported, and finding out too late, as many women do, that it is the toughest possible way of getting a living?" (*FF,* 210).

The woman of the future that Fanny Fern envisions "will marry, when she does marry, for love and companionship . . . *not* for bread and meat and clothes." Unmarried women and widows will become bookkeepers, architects, writers, and businesswomen; they will pass "through any one of the open doors through which the light of woman's millennium is shining" (*GS,* 266). One of the "open doors" is medicine, and although Fern applauded the success of women doctors, she confesses to the "narrow prejudice" of not wanting to be a patient of one of them. "My wrist reposes more comfortably in a big hand than a little one, and if my mouth is to be inspected, I prefer submitting it to a beard than to a flounce." Her "narrow prejudice" springs from a çurious distrust of women doctors' ability to be objective: "Before swallowing her pills (of which she would be the first), I should want to make sure that I had never come between her and a lover, or a new bonnet, or been the innocent recipient of a gracious smile from her husband" (*FL,* 111–12).

When it came to women having the vote, however, Fanny Fern had no such reservations. By the mid-1860s, when she was asked about this issue, her answer was "most assuredly," declaring herself to be "heart and soul" with those fighting for female suffrage (*FF,* 65). She takes issue with editorials that oppose women voting, expressing "real disappointment at their immaturity, their flippancy, their total lack of manliness" (*GS,* 75). Patriarchal attempts to prevent women from voting she viewed as just so much "boyish pop-gun firing into the air" (*GS,* 77). She deals sarcastically with the editor of an unidentified New York newspaper, who "is always throwing a blanket over a woman's head, for fear that she will see a ballot-box," and in response to his argument that women would lose their purity if they became thus involved in politics, she parodies the editor's condescension: "You may make soup, my dear, graciously says he, for poor women; or flannel shirts for very little paupers, if you'll promise not to burn your fingers in politics. That'll never do, my dear! It is *not* coarse for you to scramble at a matinee for seats, and elbow and jostle, and push men's hats awry—oh, no! that's legitimate—but to subject yourself to this kind of thing at the ballot-box, would be to forfeit men's love, and soil both your skirts and reputation" (*GS,* 80). In another column, responding to the same argument, she states, "I think a woman may vote and yet be a refined, and lady-like, and intelligent person, and worthy of all respect from those who hold womanhood in the highest esteem" (*FF,* 66).

In addition to the argument that voting would somehow sully "pure womanhood" was the paradoxical argument that women were not sensible enough to vote and that before being allowed the vote they should demonstrate moderation in their dress and behavior. This argument, too, Fanny Fern vehemently denounced as nonsense, pointing out that men were not subjected to similar tests of their fitness for voting. Describing the type of young bully and ruffian she found so annoying in the streets of New York, she remarks on his suitability as a part of the political process: "What this boy will be as a man, it is not difficult to tell. He counts one at the ballot-box, remember that, when you deny cultivated, intelligent, loyal *women* a vote there" (*FF,* 197). And while acknowledging that some women could exercise more moderation in their habits, she maintains that "it is a poor rule that won't work both ways," and offers some guidelines for the male voter: "Let him smoke 'moderately.' Let him drink 'moderately.' Let him drive 'moderately.' Let him stock-gamble 'moderately.' Let him stay out all night 'moderately.' Let him, in short, prepare himself by a severe training in the virtue of 'moderation' for the privilege of casting a vote" (*CS,* 52–53). Fanny Fern's practice of turning men's antisuffrage arguments back on them was one used by a succession of proponents of female suffrage in the ensuing years. One example that seems remarkably similar to Fern is from Alice Duer Miller's 1915 book *Are Women People? A Book of Rhymes for Suffrage Times.* In "Why We Oppose Votes for Men," Miller, like Fern, identifies and finds absurd the tenets of the political double standard:

1. Because man's place is in the armory.
2. Because no really manly man wants to settle any question otherwise than by fighting about it.
3. Because if men should adopt peaceable methods women will no longer look up to them.
4. Because men will lose their charm if they slip out of their natural sphere and interest themselves in other matters than feats of arms, uniforms, and drums.

5. Because men are too emotional to vote. Their conduct at baseball games and political conventions shows this, while their innate tendency to appeal to force renders them peculiarly unfit for the task of government.[3]

It was the contemplation of such behavior on the part of men that motivated Fanny Fern to remark that *"through her* the ballot-box is to become regenerated" (*FF,* 66).

Fanny Fern

In addition to demonstrating her stances on social issues of the midnineteenth century, Fanny Fern's later collections of columns also reveal much about her activities and enthusiasms during the last 16 years of her life. She told her reading public about her travels, her reading, Robert Bonner's stable, her penchant for freshly sharpened pencils, and the fact that she was forgetful. So completely is Sara Willis Parton absorbed by the Fanny Fern *persona* that she several times refers to her husband as "Mr. Fern." The picture that emerges is of a well-educated, energetic woman who moved in a social circle that included Robert Bonner and Horace Greeley, who went to plays and concerts, and who could afford to spend her summers in the country.

With the exception of trips to Baltimore and Richmond, most of Fanny Fern's travel took place in the Northeast, and most—apart from the summers spent in Newport—was to cities: Boston, Philadelphia, Washington, and Montreal. In addition to noting her reactions to the sights that would have attracted most tourists of the day, she was fond of commenting on the quality of the food, the condition of the streets, and the demeanor of the inhabitants. She was not fond of Montreal, despite its magnificent cathedral and its solid look because "one likes beauty as much as strength, and my eye ached for something ornamental in the way of flower-gardens" (*CS,* 201). Quebec, visited on the same trip, is far preferable, in part because of the healthy-looking, sensibly dressed women she sees, who mind their own business rather than judging other women's dress: "nobody scrutinized you as they do in New York, fixing a stony stare upon you (I speak of the New York women), till they have found out everything you have on, how it is made and trimmed" (*CS,* 208). Southern cities fare worst in Fanny Fern's travel accounts, both because of her memories of the Civil War and because the war-ravaged economy of the South precluded the amenities to which she was accustomed: "Whoso essays to travel South . . . leaves hope and comfort behind. . . . Farewell to clean rooms, and *genuine* coffee, and well-cooked meats, and prompt attendance; and welcome drafts, and cooked poison, in every shape that the fiend of the gridiron and frying-pan could devise" (*GS,* 247). Baltimore is a clean, lovely exception, and she is able to overlook their political differences, but she calls Norfolk "Sleepy Hollow," and writes that she "can't conceive of keeping awake there, unless by help of their corduroy pavements" (*GS,* 246–47). Her reaction to Richmond is immediately negative: "Lord! what a place for two big armies to fight about! . . . Amid remains of former splendor, dilapidation and stagnation reign" (*GS,* 248–49).

Born in Maine and raised in Boston, Fanny Fern throughout her life wrote of her pride in being a New Englander. She viewed the people of New England as thrifty, hardworking, clean, and sensible—all qualities that she held in high esteem. In "My Summers in New England," a rhapsodic piece about the glories of the region and its people, she comments: "I pity a genuine New Englander, who migrates from a land in which every inhabitant is born with a faculty of doing everything in the best manner, and in the very "nick of time," and settles down among a Penelope race, who weave their webs in the morning, only to find them irretrievably unravelled every night" (*FF,* 166).

Along with New England efficiency, however, went a certain amount of smugness. In her many comparisons of Boston and New York, Fern was quick to acknowledge the snobbishness of the former city. If New York was bustling, dirty, and crowded, Boston was "a snob of the first water," and she believed that some compromise between Bostonian righteousness and New York boisterousness could produce a better city than either. She advised Boston to "migrate betimes to New York; where it will get wholesomely thumped and bumped, and its conservative corns pounced upon by the rushing crowd" (*FF,* 183–84)—a progress that suggests her own move from writing sentimental prose for Boston papers to writing irreverent columns for the liberal *New York Ledger.* Of all the places that Fanny Fern traveled to from New York, Newport was her favorite, and she wrote often of its beauty and serenity. James Parton reports in his *Memorial Volume* that the last piece she wrote before her death—or, rather, dictated to him—was about "dear, blessed Newport" (*MV,* 80–81).

Newport was the summer home of a number of writers and intellectuals, some of whom became close friends of the Partons, but, with the exception of Robert Bonner and Henry Ward Beecher, Fanny Fern seldom wrote about her friends and only occasionally about her reading; hers was neither a gossip column nor a book review column. The columns that she did devote to books and authors, however, are revealing. The two authors she championed most vigorously were Walt Whitman and Charlotte Brontë, praising Whitman's *Leaves of Grass* and defending Brontë against critics who, has they had with Fern's novel *Ruth Hall,* addressed themselves to the gender of the author rather than to the book. In "In the Dumps" she traces her bad mood to a Boston reviewer's having called Brontë's novel *Jane Eyre* an "immoral book." Calling the reviewer a "donkey," she comments that "it is vain to hope that *his* life has been as pure and self-sacrificing as that of 'Charlotte Brontë'" (*FL,* 249). After reading Elizabeth Gaskell's 1857 biography of Brontë, she writes a column about "noble Charlotte Brontë, one of "earth's gifted," comparing her to a bird struggling to fly against the wind, "singing feebly its quivering notes as if to keep up its courage" (*FL,* 332). She feels intense anger at critics' charges that Brontë's work was "unwomanly" (*FL,* 334), and in a column titled "Facts for Unjust Critics" she quotes passages from the Gaskell biography that she wishes were "pasted up in editorial offices throughout the length and breadth of the land," including the following: "She, Miss Bronte, especially disliked the lowering of the standard by which to judge a work of fiction if it proceeded from a feminine pen; and praise, mingled with pseudo-gallant allusions to her sex, mortified her far more than actual blame. . . . 'I wish all reviewers believed me to be a man; they would be more just to me'" (*FL,* 297–98). Even if Fanny Fern had not been an ardent admirer of *Jane Eyre,* such sentiments would have struck deep chords in her.

If Fern felt gratified by what she found in Gaskell's *Life of Charlotte Brontë,* quite the opposite was true of *The Confidential Letters of Napoleon and Josephine,* which only served to confirm her contempt for Napoleon's treatment of Josephine. She takes issue with what the "Napoleon-mad author" of the book claims the letters show—"His *heart* is here revealed": "I suggest to Mr. Abbot (for whom, apart from this extraordinary hallucination, I have a great respect), the following amendment of the above sentence, viz.: his *want of heart* is here revealed" (*FL,* 74). She has been fascinated enough with the book to read it in one sitting, but, "as do stimulants generally," it has given her a "villainous headache" (*FL,* 74).

It seems fitting to conclude this discussion of Fanny Fern's collections of columns for the *New York Ledger* with mention of her public exchanges with Henry Ward Beecher, minister-brother of Catharine Beecher and Harriet Beecher Stowe. Beecher was Fanny Fern's contemporary, born in

1813; he was a man whom she admired, as she did his sisters. Further, the columns in which she addresses him testify to her own popularity, they contain some of her sprightliest prose, and they deal with one of her pet peeves: giving candy to children. The earlier of the two columns, "A Sermon for the Plymouth Pulpit," jocularly chastizes Beecher for advocating giving candy to children. She approaches him as one grandparent to another, acknowledging that it is difficult to say "no" to a grandchild, yet claiming that her grandchild is healthier for being denied candy. She comments that she has "worn out several pens and distributed much ink in the crusade against [candy]," only to be undermined by Beecher's pro-candy statements in the *Ledger*, "right under my very nose." The issue becomes one of gender, as Fanny Fern claims that men may give children candy, but it is women who must deal with the ensuing stomach aches and decaying teeth. Toward the end of the column, she vows to send it off to the *Ledger* before she is tempted to "make it more respectful" to a minister; she will withstand his (mock) anger, just as a woman had recently withstood hers: "I'll take example by a rampant female at a public meeting the other night who was scolding her husband for not getting her a better seat. The distressed man laid his hand on her arm, saying, 'Hush! Here's Fanny Fern; she will hear you.' With distended nostrils, that admirable woman replied, 'I don't care for six hundred Fanny Ferns!'" (*GS*, 61–63).

The second column was occasioned by a teasing passage by Beecher in the New York *Ledger*, in which he reports having "sweets" in the form of both candy and happy grandchildren in his house. "I know," he writes, "that Fanny Fern is sorry that she ever wrote a word against candy, and stands pouting, to think that I have all the sweets on my side." "Not a bit of it," retorts Fern, and reminds him that he once pursued another kind of "sweet" when he took her for rides when she was a student at Catharine Beecher's academy. Thus having "paid [him] for [his] little public dig," she expresses her admiration for his preaching, and entreats him to move his church from Brooklyn to New York so that she can attend it. The column is signed, "Your faithful adherent, Fanny Fern" (*CS*, 108–10)— the only name by which she was known by even her closest friends.

Notes and References

Preface

1. Margo Culley, ed., *A Day at a Time: The Diary Literature of American Women from 1764 to the Present* (New York: The Feminist Press, 1985), 11–12.
2. Fanny Fern, "Try Again," in *Fresh Leaves* (New York: Mason Brothers, 1857), 301–2.

Chapter One

1. [William U. Moulton], *The Life and Beauties of Fanny Fern* (1855; reprint, New Haven, Conn.: Research Publications, 1975), 43; hereafter cited in text.
2. Mary Kelley, *Private Woman, Public Stage: Literary Domesticity in Nineteenth-Century America* (New York: Oxford University Press, 1984), 35; hereafter cited in text.
3. Mae Weintraub Zlotnik, *Fanny Fern: A Biography* (Ph.D. diss., Columbia University, 1939), 22; hereafter cited in text.
4. Fred Lewis Pattee, *The Feminine Fifties* (New York: D. Appleton–Century, 1940), 110.
5. Fanny Fern, "Leaves of Grass," in *Ruth Hall and Other Writings*, ed. Joyce W. Warren (New Brunswick, N.J.: Rutgers University Press, 1986), 275.
6. Nathaniel Hawthorne, *Letters of Hawthorne to William D. Ticknor, 1851–1864*, vol. I (Newark, N.J.: The Carteret Book Club, 1910), 78.
7. Harnett T. Kane, *Dear Dorothy Dix: The Story of a Compassionate Woman* (Garden City, N.Y.: Doubleday, 1952), 59.
8. Fanny Fern, *Shadows and Sunbeams and Other Stories*, Being the Second Series of Fern Leaves from Fanny's Port-Folio (New York: John W. Lovell, [1854]), 14; hereafter cited in text as *SS*.
9. Fanny Fern, *Fern Leaves from Fanny's Port-Folio.* (1853; reprint, Chicago: Donohue, Henneberry, 1890), 321–22; hereafter cited in text as *Leaves*.
10. Fanny Fern, "*Fresh Leaves*, by Fanny Fern," *New York Ledger*, 10 October 1857. Reprinted in *Legacy: A Journal of Nineteenth-Century American Women Writers*, 2, no. 2 (Fall 1985): 59.
11. James Parton, *A Memorial Volume of Fanny Fern* (New York: G. W. Carleton, 1873), 17; hereafter cited in text as *MV*.
12. Fanny Fern, *Fresh Leaves* (New York: Mason Brothers, 1857), 100–3; hereafter cited in text as *FL*.

13. Florence Bannard Adams, *Fanny Fern; or, A Pair of Flaming Shoes* (West Trenton, N.J.: Hermitage Press, 1966), 4; hereafter cited in text.

14. Milton Rugoff, *The Beechers: An American Family in the Nineteenth Century* (New York: Harper & Row, 1981), 48; hereafter cited in text.

15. Ethel Parton, "Fanny Fern at the Hartford Female Seminary," *New England Magazine*, vol. 30 (March/August 1901): 95; hereafter cited in text.

16. Editorial, *New York Ledger*, 14 February 1863.

17. Editorial, *New York Ledger*, 26 February 1870.

18. Various sources have discrepancies in the dates that Sara's children were born. Florence Adams, for example, reports that Mary was born in 1839 and Grace in 1840. I have chosen to use the dates recorded in Joyce W. Warren's introduction to the Rutgers University Press edition of *Ruth Hall* and in Mae Weintraub Zlotnik's Ph.D. dissertation; the source in the latter work is Abner Morse, *Genealogical Register of the Descendants of Several Ancient Puritans* (Boston: L. W. Dutton, 1861).

19. Editorial, *New York Ledger*, 26 February 1859.

20. Editorial, *New York Ledger*, 17 September 1869.

21. Ishbel Ross, *Ladies of the Press* (1936; reprint, New York: Arno Press, 1974), 40.

22. Ethel Parton, " A New York Childhood," *The New Yorker*, 13 June 1936, 32.

23. Helen Waite Papashvilly, *All the Happy Endings: A study of the domestic novel in America, the women who wrote it, the women who read it, in the nineteenth century* (New York: Harper, 1956), xvi; hereafter cited in text.

24. Ann D. Wood, "The 'Scribbling Women' and Fanny Fern: Why Women Wrote," *American Quarterly* 23, no. 1 (Spring 1971) : 9.

25. [G. H. Lewes], "A Gentle Hint to Writing Women," *Leader* 1 (1850): 189.

26. Fanny Fern, *Folly As It Flies* (New York: G. W. Carleton, 1868), 61–64; hereafter cited in text as *FF*.

27. Henry A. Beers, *Nathaniel Parker Willis* (Boston: Houghton Mifflin, 1885), 335.

28. The amount of this payment is different in various accounts of the transaction, ranging from $500 to $1,000.

29. J. C. Derby, *Fifty Years Among Authors, Books and Publishers* (New York: G. W. Carleton, 1884), 211.

30. Grace Greenwood, "Fanny Fern—Mrs. Parton," *Eminent Women of the Age; Being Narratives of the Lives and Deeds of the Most Prominent Women of the Present Generation* (Hartford, Conn.: S. M. Botts, 1868), 84; hereafter cited in text.

Chapter Two

1. Quoted in Gayle Waldrop, *Editor and Editorial Writer* (New York: 1948, 304–5. Westbrook Pegler's column "Fair Enough" was syndicated from

1933 until 1962. In 1941, he won a Pulitzer Prize for exposing corruption in several labor unions.

2. Ralph Admari, "Bonner and the *Ledger*," *American Book Collector*, vol. vi (May–June 1935) :176; Frank Luther Mott, *A History of American Magazines*, vol. I (Cambridge, Mass.: Harvard University Press, 1938), 156–57.

3. Susan Coultrap-McQuin, *Doing Literary Business: American Women Writers in the Nineteenth Century* (Chapel Hill: University of North Carolina Press, 1990), 11.

4. Elizabeth Bancroft Schlesinger, "Fanny Fern: Our Grandmothers' Mentor," *New York Historical Society Quarterly* 38 (October 1954): 512; hereafter cited in text.

Chapter Three

1. Nina Baym, *Woman's Fiction: A Guide to Novels by and about Women in America, 1820–1870* (Ithaca, N.Y.: Cornell University Press, 1978), 11–12; hereafter cited in text.

2. William C. Spengemann, *The Adventurous Muse: The Poetics of American Fiction, 1789–1900* (New Haven, Conn.: Yale University Press, 1977), 69; hereafter cited in text.

3. R. H. Hutton, "Novels by the Authoress of John Halifax," *North British Review*, 29 (1858): 474.

4. "Female Novelists," *London Review*, 1 (1860): 137.

5. Josiah Allen's Wife [Marietta Holley], *My Opinions and Betsey Bobbet's* (Hartford, Conn.: American Publishing Co., 1872), v–vi.

6. Susan S. Williams, "Widening the World: Susan Warner, Her Readers, and the Assumption of Authorship," *American Quarterly*, vol. 42, no. 4 (December 1990); 565–86.

7. Corinne Dale, "The Domestic Alternative: Beyond Feminist Criticism," in *Courage & Tools: The Florence Howe Award for Feminist Scholarship, 1974–1989*, ed. Joanne Glasgow and Angela Ingram (New York: Modern Language Association, 1990), 106.

8. Fanny Fern, *Ruth Hall: A Domestic Tale of the Present Time*, ed. Joyce W. Warren (New Brunswick, N.J.: Rutgers University Press, 1986), 13; hereafter cited in text as *RH*.

9. Susan K. Harris, *19th-Century American Women's Novels: Interpretive Strategies*. (Cambridge: Cambridge University Press, 1990), 112–13.

Chapter Four

1. Fanny Fern, *Rose Clark* (New York: Mason Brothers, 1856), 117; hereafter cited in text as *RC*.

2. Stephen Knadler, "Technology in the Garden: Romantic Art and its

Educated Expression in the Age of Emerson and Melville." (Ph.D. diss., Vanderbilt University, 1991, 227).

Chapter Five

1. Fanny Fern, *Little Ferns for Fanny's Little Friends* (Auburn, N.Y.: Miller, Orton & Mulligan, 1854), 59–61; hereafter cited in text as *LF*.
2. Monica Kiefer, *American Children through their Books, 1700–1835* (Philadelphia: University of Pennsylvania Press, 1948), 7; hereafter cited in text.
3. Alice M. Jordan, *From Rollo to Tom Sawyer and Other Papers* (Boston: The Horn Book, 1948), 14; hereafter cited in text.
4. Carolyn L. Karcher, "Lydia Maria Child and the *Juvenile Miscellany*," in *Research About Nineteenth-Century Children and Books*, ed. Selma K. Richardson (Champaign: University of Illinois Graduate School of Library Science, 1980), 67; hereafter cited in text.
5. Elva S. Smith, *The History of Children's Literature*, rev. ed. (Chicago: American Library Association, 1980), 139.
6. Julia Briggs, "Women Writers and Writing for Children: From Sarah Fielding to E. Nesbit," in *Children and Their Books*, ed. Gillian Avery and Julia Briggs (Oxford: Clarendon Press, 1989), 222.
7. Prospectus. *The Youth's Companion*, 16 April 1827, 1.
8. Anne Scott MacLeod, *A Moral Tale: Children's Fiction and American Culture, 1820–1860* (Hamden, Conn.: Archon Books, 1975), 28; hereafter cited in text.
9. Fanny Fern, *The Play-Day Book: New Stories for Little Folks* (New York: Mason Brothers, 1857), 42; hereafter cited in text as *PD*.
10. Fanny Fern, *The New Story Book for Children* (New York: Mason Brothers, 1864), 62; hereafter cited in text as *SB*.

Chapter Six

1. Fanny Fern, *Ginger-Snaps* (New York: Carleton, 1870), 32; hereafter cited in text as *GS*.
2. Fanny Fern, *Caper-Sauce; A Volume of Chit-Chat about Men, Women, and Things* (New York: G. W. Carleton, 1872); hereafter cited in text as *CS*.
3. Alice Duer Miller, "Why We Oppose Votes for Men," *Redressing the Balance: American Women's Literary Humor from Colonial Times to the 1980s*, ed. Nancy Walker and Zita Dresner (Jackson: University Press of Mississippi, 1988), 204–5.

Selected Bibliography

PRIMARY SOURCES

Novels

Rose Clark. New York: Mason Brothers, 1856.
Ruth Hall. New York: Mason Brothers, 1854.

Newspaper Columns

Caper-Sauce. New York: G. W. Carleton, 1872.
Fern Leaves from Fanny's Port-Folio. Auburn, N.Y: Derby and Miller, 1853.
Fern Leaves from Fanny's Port-Folio. Second Series. Auburn, N.Y.: Miller, Orton, and Mulligan, 1854.
Folly As It Flies. New York: G. W. Carleton, 1868.
Fresh Leaves. New York: Mason Brothers, 1857.
Ginger-Snaps. New York: G. W. Carleton, 1870.

Books for Children

Little Ferns for Fanny's Little Friends. Auburn, N.Y.: Derby and Miller, 1853.
The New Story Book for Children. New York: Mason Brothers, 1864.
The Play-Day Book. New York: Mason Brothers, 1857.

SECONDARY SOURCES

Books, Parts of Books, and Articles

Adams, Florence Bannard. *Fanny Fern; or, A Pair of Flaming Shoes*. West Trenton, N.J.: Hermitage Press, 1966. An informal, enthusiastic, occasionally inaccurate account of Fanny Fern's life and career, this 27-page pamphlet is nonetheless one of the first sources to recognize and appreciate Fern's use of humor.
Breslaw, Elaine Gellis. "Popular Pundit: Fanny Fern and the Emergence of the American Newspaper Columnist." Master's thesis, Smith College, 1956. A study of Fanny Fern's place in the development of the modern newspaper columnist.

Greenwood, Grace. "Fanny Fern—Mrs. Parton," *Eminent Women of the Age*. Hartford, Conn.: S. M. Botts, 1868, 66–84. An affectionate portrait of Fanny Fern written by a contemporary and friend.

Harris, Susan K. *19th-Century American Women's Novels: Interpretive Strategies*. Cambridge: Cambridge University Press, 1990, 111–27. A very fine analysis of Fanny Fern's use of multiple "voices" in *Ruth Hall*.

Kelley, Mary. *Private Woman, Public Stage: Literary Domesticity in Nineteenth-Century America*. New York: Oxford University Press, 1984. Fanny Fern is one of the writers included in Kelley's excellent study of the tension between the public and private identities of nineteenth-century American women writers.

[William U. Moulton]. *The Life and Beauties of Fanny Fern*. 1855. New Haven, Conn.: Research Publications, 1975. An anonymously published "biography" of Fanny Fern, identifying the author of *Ruth Hall* as Sara Willis and chastising her for her unflattering portraits of members of her family in the novel. The book is now presumed to have been written by the editor of the Boston *True Flag*, and it includes a number of columns originally written for that newspaper.

Parton, Ethel. "Fanny Fern at the Hartford Female Seminary," *New England Magazine* 30 (March/August 1901): 94–98. An account of Sara Willis's years at Catharine Beecher's school, drawing on family documents, written by Fanny Fern's granddaughter.

———. "A Little Girl and Two Authors," *The Horn Book* (March–April 1941): 81–86. Fanny Fern's granddaughter reminisces about her childhood with the Partons, indicating that her grandmother put her theories of childrearing into practice.

———. "A New York Childhood." *The New Yorker* 13 June 1936: 32–46. Fanny Fern's granddaughter reminisces about her childhood after being adopted by Sara and James Parton.

Parton, James. *A Memorial Volume of Fanny Fern*. New York: G. W. Carleton, 1873. The volume includes an affectionate biographical sketch by Fanny Fern's third husband and a number of her newspaper columns.

Pattee, Fred Lewis. *The Feminine Fifties*. New York: D. Appleton-Century, 1940. Pattee's study was one of the earliest to address women's fiction of the 1850s, but it also perpetuated the erroneous view that Fanny Fern's work was uniformly sentimental.

Ross, Ishbel. *Ladies of the Press*. 1936. New York: Arno Press, 1974. In this anecdotal history of women in American journalism, Ross devotes a brief chapter to Fanny Fern.

Schlesinger, Elizabeth Bancroft. "Fanny Fern: Our Grandmothers' Mentor," *New York Historical Society Quarterly* 38 (October 1954): 501–19. A brief analysis of some of the topics of Fanny Fern's newspaper columns, emphasizing her appeal to a large female readership.

————. "Proper Bostonians as Seen by Fanny Fern," *New England Quarterly* 27 (March 1954): 97–102. An informal analysis of Fanny Fern's mixed attitudes toward the city in which she grew up.

Warren, Joyce W. *Fanny Fern: An Independent Woman.* New Brunswick: Rutgers University Press, 1992. The first full-length biography of Fanny Fern, written by the scholar who edited *Ruth Hall* for re-publication in 1986.

Wood, Ann D. "The 'Scribbling Women' and Fanny Fern: Why Women Wrote," *American Quarterly* 23 (Spring 1971): 3–24. Predating Kelley's *Private Woman, Public Stage,* Wood's article explores the motivations for women to become authors in the mid-nineteenth century, emphasizing Fanny Fern's antidomestic stance.

Zlotnik, Mae Weintraub. "Fanny Fern: A Biography." Master's thesis, Columbia University, 1939. Zlotnik relies uncritically on Moulton's spurious "biography," but the thesis is otherwise a fairly reliable source of biographical information.

Index

Alcott, Louisa May, 83
Alger, Horatio, 46, 85, 92
"All About the Dolans," 89
American Sunday School Union, 81–82
American Way of Death, The (Mitford), 112
"And Ye Shall Call the Sabbath a Delight," 107–8
"Angel in the House" (Woolf), 39
Appeal in Favor of that Class of Americans Called Africans, An (Child), 83
Are Women People? A Book of Rhymes for Suffrage Times (Miller), 118
Atlas (New York), 19
"Aunt Fanny," 85–86, 92–93, 95
"Aunt Hetty on Matrimony," 35
"Awe-ful Thoughts," 106

"Bachelor Housekeeping," 31
"Bald Eagle," 94
Barbauld, Anna, 82
Beecher, Catharine, 7–9, 84, 111, 121–22
Beecher, Henry Ward, 120–22
Beecher, Lyman, 7–8
Beers, Henry A., 17
"Bessie and her Mother," 94
"Best Things," 38
Blackwell's Island, 110
"Blue Monday," 115
Bonaparte, Napoleon, 121
Bonner, Robert, 19–22, 24–25, 47, 99–100, 119–20
"Borrowed Light," 4–5
Boston Recorder, 6
Bowles, Samuel, 23–24
"Breakfast at the Paxes," 104
"Bridget as She Was, and Bridget as She Is," 109
Brontë, Charlotte, 96, 121
Brontë, Emily, 96
Brown, John, 97

Bryant, William Cullen, 20, 25
Buchwald, Art, 23
Burns, Robert, 95
Burr, Aaron, 18
"Business Man's Home, A," 105
Byron, George Gordon Lord, 95–96

Caper-Sauce, 4, 20, 101
"Chapter on Literary Women, A," 29–30
"Charity Orphans, The," 87
Child, Lydia Maria, 82–83
"Children have their Rights," 71
"Children in 1853," 89
children's literature, development of, 80–84
"Cicely Hunt; or, The Lame Girl," 86
"Circus, The," 93
"City Scenes and City Life," 37–38
Civil War, 72, 81, 83, 97, 101, 112–13, 119–20
Clarissa Harlowe (Richardson), 81
Color Purple, The (Walker), 50
"Come on, MacDuff," 100
Confidential Letters of Napoleon and Josephine, The (Abbot), 121
Cooper, James Fenimore, 44
Cotton, John, 81
"Country Diet," 112
"Crazy Tim," 87–88
"Critics," 39
Curse of Clifton, The (Southworth), 42

"Dark Days," 26
"Delightful Men," 114–15
Derby, J. C., 17–18
Dickens, Charles, 19, 21, 25, 59
Dickinson, Emily, 23
"Discourse Upon Husbands, A," 106
Dix, Dorothy, 3
Dodge, Mary Mapes, 98

"Dollars and Dimes," 56
domestic novel, 40–45
Dyer, Oliver, 17

Eastern Argus (Portland, Maine), 5, 23
Edgeworth, Maria, 82
"Edith May," 32–34
"Editors," 30
Eldredge, Charles Harrington, 10–12, 15, 18, 84, 106
Eldredge, Ellen Willis, 11, 13, 18, 21
Eldredge, Grace Harrington, 11, 15, 18, 20
Eldredge, Hezekiah, 10
Eldredge, Mary 11
Evans, Augusta, 42
Everett, Edward, 19
"Everybody's Vacation Except Editors," 30–31

"Facts for Unjust Critics," 121
"Fair Play," 109
"Fanny Ford; A Story of Everyday Life," 102–3, 110
Farrington, Samuel P., 12–14, 17, 33, 75–76, 114
"Fashionable Preacher, The," 38
Feminine Mystique, The (Friedan), 16
Fern, Fanny (Sara Payson Willis Parton), childhood, 6–7; education, 7–10; marriage: to Charles Eldredge, 10–12; to Samuel P. Farrington, 12–14, 75–76, 114; to James Parton, 18, 20–21; views on: advice manuals, 105; child-rearing, 89, 94, 103, 121; city vs. country life, 37–38; diet, 111–12; education, 58–59, 70–71, 95, 110–11; fashion and clothing reform, 57, 106–7, 108–9; funerals, 112; immigrants, 88–89; marriage, 32, 34–36, 45, 67–68, 78, 105–6, 114–15; materialism, 56–57, 71–73, 86–87; motherhood, 33, 35–36, 96; prison reform, 103, 110; religion and the clergy, 28–29, 52–53, 73–74, 106–8; temperance, 91–92, 97; wife abuse, 32–33, 36–37, 75–78; women as writers, 4–5, 27, 29–31, 38–

39, 46–47, 60–61, 78–79, 104, 121; women's rights, 33–34, 113–19
"Fern Leaves," 2, 26, 36, 102, 104–5, 110, 115
Fern Leaves from Fanny's Port-Folio, 4, 11, 17, 19–21, 25–35, 45, 90
Fern Leaves, Second Series, 4, 11, 20, 25, 35–39
"Fern Soliloquy, A," 28–29
Fish, Hamilton, 20
Folly As It Flies, 4, 16, 20, 71, 99, 107
Franklin, Benjamin, 18
Fresh Leaves, 4, 6, 20, 100, 102
Friedan, Betty, 16
"Frontier Life," 88
"Fun and Folly; A Story for Thoughtless Boys," 94

Gaskell, Elizabeth, 121
"Gauntlet for the Men, A," 114
"Gentle Hint to Writing Women, A" (Lewes), 16
Gilligan, Carol, 58
Ginger-Snaps, 4, 20
"Give the Convicts a Chance," 110
"Glance at a Chameleon Subject, A," 109
Godey's Lady's Book, 83
Goodman, Ellen, 23
"Grandfather Glen," 33
Greeley, Horace, 18–20, 23–24, 92–93, 119
Greenwood, Grace, 20–30
Guardian of Education, The (Trimmer), 82
Gulliver's Travels (Swift), 81

Hale, Sarah Josepha, 15, 83
Harte, Bret, 20
Hartford Female Seminary, 7–10, 122
"Have We Any Men Among Us?" 39
Hawthorne, Nathaniel, 2–3, 15–16, 44
"Hetty's Mistake," 88
Hidden Hand, The (Southworth), 42
"History of a Family of Cats," 91
"History of Our Late War, The," 113
"Hod-Carrier, The," 93
Hogarth, William, 37
Holley, Marietta, 43, 104, 116

Home Journal (New York), 17–18
Household Tyrants (Thackeray), 36–37
"How Husbands May Rule," 32
"How Woman Loves," 32
Huck Finn, 41, 83
"Huswifery" (Taylor), 44
Hutton, R. H., 43

"In the Dumps," 121
Independent Chronicle (Boston), 5
"Inventor of the Locomotive, The," 98

Jackson, Andrew, 18, 95, 97
Jane Eyre (C. Brontë), 121
Janeway, James, 81
Jefferson, Thomas, 18
Johnson, Samuel, 95, 97
Journal (New York), 3
"Journey, The," 90, 93
"Justice for Ministers," 107
Juvenile Miscellany, The, 82

Kingston, Maxine Hong, 50
"Knickerbocker and Tri-Mountain," 108–9

Landers, Ann, 104
"Last Bachelor Hours of Tom Pax, The,"
    106
Leaves of Grass (Whitman), 3, 121
Lessons for Children (Barbauld), 82
"Letter from Tom Grimalkin to his
    Mother," 91
Lewes, George Henry, 16
Life and Beauties of Fanny Fern, The, 1–2,
    12, 14, 19, 39
Life of Charlotte Brontë (Gaskell), 121
"Literary Aspirants," 100
"Literary People," 100
"Little Bunker Hill, A," 34
"Little Dandelion Merchant, The," 80, 85
Little Ferns for Fanny's Little Friends, 18–
    19, 80, 84–89, 90–91, 94
"Little Floy," 89
Little Henry and His Bearer (Sherwood), 82
"Little Lord, The," 96
"Little Martyr, The," 89
"Little Musician, The," 92

"Little Sisters, The," 91–92
"Little Tambourine Player, The," 89
Longfellow, Henry Wadsworth, 19, 25
Lord Chesterfield, 96–97
"Lost and the Living, The," 33
"Lucky Irish Boy, A," 93

"Mary Lee," 32, 34
Mason Brothers, 4, 19
Massachusetts State Prison, 110
Melville, Herman, 44
Memorial Volume of Fanny Fern (Parton), 9,
    14, 21, 120
Merchants' Ledger and Statistical Review
    (New York), 19, 24
Miller, Alice Duer, 118
Mitford, Jessica, 112
Moby-Dick (Melville), 44
"Model Husband, A," 36
"Model Minister, The," 17
"Model Step-Mother, The," 33
"Model Widower, The," 3
"Moral Molasses; or, Too Sweet by Half,"
    105
Mother's Assistant, The, 17
Moulton, William, 1–2, 13–14, 39
"Mrs. Adolphus Smith Sporting the 'Blue
    Stocking,' " 39
"Mrs. Grundy," 110
"Mrs. Weasel's Husband," 36
Musical World and Times (New York), 17,
    19, 25
"My First Convert," 101
"My Old Ink-Stand and I; or, The First
    Column in the New House," 101–2
My Opinions and Betsey Bobbet's (Holley),
    116
"My Summers in New England," 120

"New Cook, The," 87–88
New Story Book for Children, The 20, 80, 84,
    95–98
New York Evening Mirror, 24
New York Herald, 99
"New-York in Shadow," 88
New York Ledger, 7, 9–11, 19–21, 24–25,

31, 47, 99–100, 102–3, 110, 112,
    120–22
New Yorker, The, 13, 20, 36–37
newspaper column, development of, 23–25

"Old Hickory," 97
"Old Maid of the Period, The," 116
Olive Branch (Boston), 14, 16–17, 25
"Our Hatty," 30
"Our Nelly," 37

"Page from a Woman's Heart, A," 28
Pamela (Richardson), 81
Parent's Assistant, The (Edgeworth), 82
Parker, Dorothy, 36
Parker, Hannah, 5, 11
Parton, Ethel, 8, 13, 20–21, 84
Parton, James, 6, 9, 13–15, 18, 20–21, 39,
    95, 106, 120
Parton, Sara Payson Willis. See Fern, Fanny
"Passionate Father, The," 33
Payson, Edward, 5–6, 107
"Peep Under Ground, A," 89
Pegler, Westbrook, 24
Pierre (Melville), 70
Play-Day Book, The, 20, 80, 90–95
"Ploughboy Poet, The," 97
Poe, Edgar Allan, 44
"Poor-Rich Child, The," 92
Portland Gazette (Maine), 5, 23
"Practical Blue-Stocking, The," 29
"Prophet's Chamber, The," 28
Punch, 36
"Puss and I," 91
"Question, and its Answer, A," 104
"Question Answered, A," 95

Rose Clark, 14, 63–79, 80, 87, 94, 102
Ruth Hall, 1–2, 4, 6, 11–20, 25–28, 39,
    40–62, 63, 65–66, 68–69, 71, 73–76,
    78–79, 121; critical reception of, 1–2,
    4, 18–19, 61–62

St. Nicholas magazine, 98
Saturday Evening Post, 19
Sedgwick, Catharine, 42
"Self-Conquest," 27–28, 45

Seneca Falls Woman's Rights Convention,
    34, 41
"Sermon for the Plymouth Pulpit, A," 122
Shadows and Sunbeams. See Fern Leaves, Sec-
    ond Series
Sherwood, Martha, 82
Sigourney, Lydia, 19, 25
"Sin of Being Sick, The," 111
"Soliloquy of Mr. Broadbrim," 38–39
"Some Gossip About Myself," 104
"Some Varieties of Women," 113–14
Sorosis, 21
Southworth, E.D.E.N., 25, 40, 42
Spiritual Milk for Babes (Cotton), 81
Springfield Republican (Massachusetts), 23
"Step-Mother, The," 33
Stephen, M.D. (Warner), 44
"Story About Myself, A," 95
"Story for Boys, A," 94
Stowe, Harriet Beecher, 8–9, 15, 25, 121
"Street-Scene," 86
"Suggestions on Arithmetic," 9
"Summer Days; or, The Young Wife's Af-
    fliction," 26
"Sunday in the Village," 107
"Sunshine and Young Mothers," 35–36

"Talk of the Town" (The New Yorker), 37
Taylor, Edward, 44
"Tear of a Wife, The," 34
"Temperance Story, A," 92
Tennyson, Alfred Lord, 19, 25
Terhune, Mary Virginia, 25
Thackeray, William, 36
Thoreau, Henry David, 108
"Thorns for the Rose," 26–27
"To Young Girls," 104–5
Token for Children, A (Janeway), 81
"Tom-Boy, The," 94
Tom Jones (Fielding), 81
Tom Sawyer, 83
Trimmer, Sarah K., 82
True Flag (Boston), 1, 14, 17, 25
Twain, Mark, 3, 83

"Uncle Ben's Attack of Spring Fever, and
    How He Got Cured," 38

Uncle Tom's Cabin (Stowe), 9
"Unwritten History of the War, The,"
   113

van Buren, Abigail, 104

Walker, Alice, 50
War of 1812, 5
Warner, Susan, 15, 42–44, 48
"Weaker Vessel, The," 34
"What Shall We Do for the Little Children on Sunday?" 108
White, E. B., 36
Whitman, Walt, 3, 121
Whittier, John Greenleaf, 19
"Who is Rich?—Who is Poor?" 86–87
"Who Would be the Last Man," 36
"Why We Oppose Votes for Men"
   (Miller), 118

Wide, Wide World (Warner), 42–44
"Widow's Trials, The," 27
"Wild Rose, The," 94
Willis, George, 5
Willis, Nathaniel, 1, 5–7, 10–12, 23, 82
Willis, N. P., 1, 17–18
"Woman's Millennium," 115
Woman Warrior, The (Kingston), 50
"Women and Money," 37
"Women and Some of Their Mistakes,"
   113
"Women and Their Discontents," 114
"Women on the Platform," 116
Woolf, Virginia, 39
"Word to Parents and Teachers, A," 111
"Writing 'Compositions,'" 111

Youth's Companion, The, 6, 10, 82, 84

The Author

Nancy A. Walker is Director of Women's Studies and Professor of English at Vanderbilt University. A native of Louisiana, she received her B.A. from Louisiana State University and her M.A. from Tulane University. After receiving her Ph.D. from Kent State University in 1971, she taught American literature, American Studies, and Women's Studies at Stephens College, where she also served as Assistant to the President and Chair of the Department of Languages and Literature.

A specialist in American women writers, Walker is the author of *A Very Serious Thing: Women's Humor and American Culture* (1988) and *Feminist Alternatives: Irony and Fantasy in the Contemporary Novel by Women* (1990), which won the first annual Eudora Welty Prize. She has published numerous articles in such journals as *American Quarterly, Tulsa Studies in Women's Literature, American Literature,* and *American Literary Realism,* and several essays on women's autobiography. With Zita Dresner, she edited *Redressing the Balance: American Women's Literary Humor from the Colonial Period to the 1980s* (1988).

Walker currently serves as general editor for the period 1800–1914 for Twayne's United States Authors Series and is editing a new critical edition of Kate Chopin's *The Awakening* for St. Martin's Press.